REAL ESTATE NEUROSCIENCE

REAL ESTATE NEUROSCIENCE

THE MISSING PIECE THE GURUS DON'T TEACH

JASON GOBELI

Jason Gobeli
Real Estate Neuroscience
The Missing Piece the Gurus Don't Teach

Published by Spines
ISBN: 979-8-90222-796-0

LEGAL NOTICE & DISCLAIMER

This book is intended for educational and informational purposes only.
It does not constitute legal, financial, investment, tax, or medical advice.
The author is not acting as an attorney, CPA, financial advisor, securities broker, or medical professional.

Real estate investing involves risk, including the possible loss of principal.
Readers should conduct their own due diligence, consult qualified professionals, and comply with all federal, state, and local laws before making any financial decisions.

Examples, personal stories, strategies, and scenarios described in this book are for illustration only and may not be suitable for your situation.
Past performance is not indicative of future results.
No guarantees or promises of income, profit, or success are being made or implied.

This book discusses certain real estate investment strategies that may involve legal, tax, or regulatory considerations, including but not limited to securities regulations, syndications, private placements, partnership structures, and creative financing.
Readers should consult with licensed attorneys, CPAs, and qualified advisors before using any such strategies.

Any references to hypnosis, neurolinguistic programming (NLP), mindset practices, or subconscious techniques are for personal development purposes only and are not intended to diagnose, treat, or cure any psychological or medical condition.
Individuals with mental health concerns should consult qualified healthcare professionals.

By reading this book, you acknowledge and accept full responsibility for your decisions and actions.
The author, publisher, and affiliates disclaim all liability for any loss, damage, or adverse outcome resulting from the use or application of the information contained herein.

TABLE OF CONTENTS

FOREWORD

Are you ready to get your career — and your life — on track?

Are you ready to be truly honest with yourself about what's been holding you back, not just in real estate, but in your everyday relationships?

I have had the distinct pleasure of knowing Jason Gobeli for more than four decades. Jason and I started out together in the car business when I was a totally green 21-year-old with just $200 in my pocket. Jason showed me the power of working hard, working smart, and learning to close the deal. Under his mentorship, I became a strong salesperson — strong enough to launch a career that would eventually take me to the very top of the automotive industry.

From those early dealership days, I went on to become the owner of a Mercedes-Benz dealership and later purchased a struggling Jaguar Land Rover store in Los Angeles — ultimately building it into the #1 Jaguar Land Rover dealership in the United States. I grew that company into a valuation of more than $100 million before selling it in 2022 and writing my own bestselling book, Driven to Succeed.

I can say without hesitation:

the principles Jason shares in this book helped shape my success — both in business and in life.

I still use the mindset, disciplines, and strategies he teaches today in my real estate investments.

But here is what truly sets this book apart — **FFL: Faith, Forgiveness, and Love.**

Without FFL, what do we really have?

This is the foundation that makes Jason's approach different. When you bring Faith, Forgiveness, and Love into your career — especially into real estate, where relationships are everything — the results are transformational.

You will see the changes.

You will feel the changes.

You will build deeper, more meaningful connections with the people you serve.

Jason has not only written a guide to winning in real estate — he has written a blueprint for living a fuller, more successful, more aligned life.

As you begin this powerful book, be prepared for growth, breakthrough, and a renewed sense of purpose in everything you do.

To your future success — in business, and beyond.

Scott Biehl
Entrepreneur | Real Estate Investor | MSA Specialist
Former Owner of the #1 Jaguar Land Rover Dealership in the United States
Bestselling Author of Driven to Succeed
Founder & Managing Partner, Luminova Capital

INTRODUCTION

I've walked through a lot of rough properties in my life. Not the pretty ones they show on the TV flip shows. I'm talking about the real deal.

Houses where I had to hold my breath because there was pet feces all over the floor.
Places where water was dripping through the ceiling.
Walls marked with gang symbols.
Squatters living in attics.

They say every home tells a story, but some of the homes I've walked through have definitely been horror stories. I'd ask myself:

"How could someone let it get this bad?"

Most people take one look and they're gone —
way too many headaches,
way too much work,
no way it can be worth the effort.

I've learned something over the years, not only as a real estate guy, but as someone who has had to rebuild my own life more than once:

A damaged house isn't worthless.
It just needs someone who can see its potential beyond the mess.

In legal terms, when a house becomes this deteriorated, it's called "degradation." It means "of no value" or "useless."

There have been times in my life when I felt exactly like that.

If that house had feelings, I'd know what it was experiencing.

I remember a time — as clear as if it were yesterday — where my life was a mess. Everything felt like it was falling apart. Financially. Emotionally. Spiritually. All of it… just ripped away. And this was after seasons of success.

I've been there.

And just like when I walk into one of those houses, I looked at my own life and thought:

"Is this even salvageable?"

I wasn't born an author with multiple books.
I wasn't born a guy who trained hundreds of salespeople.
I wasn't born owning property in four states, giving seminars, writing hypnosis programs, or running a real estate brokerage.

I grew up poor.
In a small town.
My father died before I became a teenager.

I've walked through pain that felt like a kick in the gut.

During those low points, I questioned everything. I didn't trust my own judgment. I didn't even like myself. But I've learned this:

When you strip everything down — all the drywall, all the distractions — you finally see what's really there.

Underneath the damage…
there is potential.
There is value.

There is identity and character.
There is something to rebuild.

And that's where transformation begins.

It takes time.
It takes humility.
It takes courage.
It takes faith.
It takes a whole lot of emotional elbow grease.

It isn't easy letting go of what once was —
but it's worth it.
And that's what love is all about:
doing the work to make things right.

One step at a time.

That's exactly how the FFL Wealth System was born. Not from theory. Not from a seminar. You can't go to school for this stuff.

You learn it from losing.
From hurting.
From rebuilding.
From healing.

So why am I telling you all of this in a book about real estate?

Because after years of teaching seminars, negotiating deals, coaching people, training investors, and changing lives, I realized something the gurus never talk about:

Real estate is only 20% numbers...and 80% about the person running the numbers.

Anyone can learn cap rates, cash flow, DSCR, underwriting — and you will learn those things in this book.

But none of that matters if:

your beliefs are misaligned,
your confidence is shaky,
your past is still weighing you down,
your energy is low,
your identity is confused,
or you're surrounded by the wrong people.

Most people don't fail because they're incapable.
They fail because they sabotage themselves without even knowing it.

They hesitate.
They overthink.
They under-offer.
They get involved with the wrong partners.
They talk themselves out of opportunities.

It's not because they're weak.
It's not because they're untalented.
It's not because they're unlucky.

It's because they're misaligned.

And alignment is EVERYTHING.

Most people think success comes from finding the perfect deal.
I'm here to tell you:

Success comes from becoming the person who creates the perfect deal.

You don't need to become someone else —
you need to become the best version of YOU.

You need your strength.
Your vision.
Your resilience.
Your faith.
Your ability to forgive yourself.
Your ability to love yourself enough to take the next step.

Just like that beat-up house, the value was always there.
It was just waiting for someone to have faith in it.

And that's what Real Estate Neuroscience is about.

It's about building YOU so you can build wealth.

Sure, you'll learn the math, the strategies, deal evaluation, raising capital, negotiation, partnerships — all of it. But none of that is more important than getting yourself right from the inside out.

Because real estate isn't the most valuable asset you have.

YOU are.

That rundown house I talked about earlier would still be rundown today if someone with vision didn't walk in and decide to transform it.

That "someone" is who you are in this story.

The FFL Wealth System isn't just about building portfolios.
It's about transformation.

It’s about legacy.

Now let’s move forward —
and learn how to build wealth ethically, powerfully, and intentionally…

the FFL way.

PART I
THE FOUNDATION
THE NEUROSCIENCE OF WEALTH

CHAPTER 1

MONEY IS JUST MATH. WEALTH IS ENERGY

Most people think money is the hard part. If you strip it all down and look at it honestly, money isn't complicated at all.

Money is math. Basic math.

Income – Expenses = Profit.

It's neutral. Predictable. Simple.

Anyone — and I mean anyone — can learn the formulas. You can watch a YouTube video, sit through a seminar, read a book, or spend twenty minutes with a calculator and understand what cash flow is.

If wealth were purely math, every college graduate, every seminar attendee, every smart person, and every spreadsheet warrior would be wealthy.

They're not.

So what's the real difference?

Why do some people take the same information and succeed… while others stay frozen, frustrated, or financially stuck?

The answer is simple:

Wealth requires more than one ingredient. It's the combo plate — not the dollar menu.

And most people don't even know what they want to order.

So let's start looking at the secret menu for real estate success.

Knowledge Alone Ain't Enough

If knowledge alone created wealth, then every seminar room would be filled with millionaires.

Walk into any room full of "students," and you'll notice something very quickly:

They know a LOT.
They learn a LOT.
They take notes.
They ask questions.
They highlight entire books.
They watch all the gurus.
They buy every course.

And then… they freeze.

It's the paralysis-by-analysis crowd.

Smart.
Well-meaning.
High intention.
No real results.

This group believes they have to know everything before doing anything. They also think they need business cards, websites, high-dollar funnels, and all kinds of tools before making that first move.

They convince themselves they're "being responsible," when really?

They're scared. Afraid of making a mistake.
They think perfection must come before progress.
They want total certainty before they take a single step.

So they study.
And study.
And study.

And yet self-doubt still keeps them stuck.

These are the people who wait for the stars to align, the timing to be perfect, the fear to disappear, and the universe to give them a written permission slip.

And that day never comes.

They're like a brand-new hammer sitting in a toolbox.

It looks nice.
Ain't building a thing.

Two People — Same Effort — Opposite Results

Then you've got the second group — the workers.

These are the hustlers.
The grinders.
The "I'll just outwork everybody" people.

Good people with strong work ethic.
And yet no matter how hard they push… they stay stuck in the same spot.

Running, running, running — like a hamster on a wheel.

They were taught hard work is the key to success. And they believe it.

You can't force your way into wealth just by sweating more than the next person.

These are the people who do, do, do, and do some more — but without the right internal alignment or the right strategy.

They're constantly busy.
Constantly moving.
Constantly exhausted.

Without direction… without help… it's just effort. The kind of effort that wears a person down emotionally, physically, and spiritually.

These are great people, and they seem to put the world on their shoulders.

Instead of getting help, or changing their mindset, they think:

"Maybe if I just work harder, I can be more successful."

That mindset is gasoline on a fire.

Because effort without direction is motion, not progress.

Don't get me wrong — action is definitely necessary.

However, if you keep rowing your boat the same way, without help, the boat turns in circles and you get nowhere.

Dreamer, Can You Put Your Hands on Your Head?

Then we have the dreamers.

I love these people.
They have beautiful hearts.
They're positive, hopeful, spiritual, kind, and full of faith.

They just live in the clouds… and their feet aren't on the ground.

These are the people who pray for a miracle… yet won't grab the life jacket when someone throws it to them.

They say:

"I believe it's coming."
"I'm manifesting success."
"The universe is aligning for me."
"Something big is about to happen."

And maybe it is — if you participate.

Mindset is powerful — it's vital — and it absolutely matters.
However, mindset alone won't build wealth.

You can't "think" yourself into financial freedom.
You can't affirm your way into a multi-family purchase.
You can't visualize your way into closing a deal you never picked up the phone for.

Faith without action and knowledge is simply daydreaming.
And in school, daydreaming kept me from learning the lesson.

These people have their heads in the right place… not their hands.

Your head might be full of belief…
your hands need to join the party.

The Magic Combination

Now here's where everything comes together.

We've looked at the three types:

The Knowledge-Only people
The Effort-Only people
The Mindset-Only people

All three groups have part of the answer.
None of them have the whole answer.

Wealth requires the combination — the trifecta — the sturdiness of a tripod.

Knowledge + Effort + Mindset = Success

Not one.
Not two.

ALL THREE.

Knowledge gives you the what.
Effort gives you the movement.
Mindset gives you the alignment.

When these three lock together — that's when wealth starts to materialize.

When you combine the right information
with the right action
and the right inner identity…

Success becomes unstoppable.

Not because you're lucky.
Not because of timing.
Not because someone else gave you a break.

It's because you've built the internal architecture that wealth sits on.

This is the real money-flow equation — and with it, you can learn how to live in its current.

Summary

So let's bring it all home:

Knowledge alone ain't enough.
We all know smart people who aren't successful.

Effort alone ain't enough.
We all know hard workers who aren't successful.

Mindset alone ain't enough.
We all know positive thinkers who aren't successful.

But when all three come together?

Knowledge + Effort + Mindset = Success.

That's the formula for the flow of money.
That's the foundation you can build on.

That's the truth nobody taught you — until now.

The next question becomes:

How do we activate all three pieces consistently? How do we stay aligned? How do we break the patterns that keep most people stuck? How do we unlock the version of ourselves capable of success?

That's exactly what we're diving into next.

It's time for Chapter 2 – How Most People Get Stuck.

CHAPTER 2
HOW MOST PEOPLE GET STUCK

You'd think that once people learn the basics — the math, the terms, the formulas — they'd move forward and start building wealth.

Many people don't move at all. And the vast majority who do get motivated, believe they're ready to make a change, start moving… gradually quit. The self-defeating beliefs sneak in, behavior patterns repeat themselves, distractions show up, life happens — and those goals get put on the back burner.

The truth is:

People don't get stuck because they're incapable or because circumstances get in the way.

They get stuck because something inside them is out of alignment— **and they sabotage themselves without even knowing it.**

Now, this chapter is NOT about blame.
It's about clarity.

As a matter of fact, when we start blaming ourselves for not sticking to it, it makes matters worse. Because if you can see what's causing you to get stuck, then you have a better chance of understanding how to break free and move forward.

So let's take a deep dive into some of these things that block us, so we can become more aware of them.

Belief Systems That Limit Action

We all grew up hearing comments that stick with us — comments we carry throughout our lives.

I remember hearing things like:

"You never finish anything."
"You're book-smart, but you have no common sense."
"Don't be greedy — it's a sin to want more."
"People like us aren't born to be rich and famous."
"You're not special. You're just like everybody else."

I'm sure you've got your own.

Those little sentences get stored as truth before we even know we're accepting them. We may even play those old tapes and not realize they're running in the background.

You can tell yourself all you want that this time will be different… but if your subconscious starts whispering in the background, you could be on the path of self-destruction in no time — especially when it sounds like your own voice.

After all, no one can tear me down like I can tear me down.

And the scary thing is: once my own voice starts repeating things like this, I'm about to board the excuse train straight into victimhood… and justify in my head why it's okay to quit.

"It's just not my time."

"I can't catch a break."
"People will be jealous if I'm successful."
"Maybe I just don't have it in me."
"Money isn't important anyway."
"I wonder if someone cursed me."

You've got to stop that negative self-talk.

Your conscious mind is trying to step forward…
while your subconscious is pulling you right back into old beliefs.

It's not your fault — it happens quietly and automatically.
It's your conditioning.

And this is why later we'll dig deep into **Forgiveness** —
not the forgiveness of others,
but forgiveness that releases the emotional weight of your past
so you can finally move freely.

Forgiveness helps you let go of the things that bind you…
even if those things have felt like your best friends your whole life.

Because how can you possibly be focused in the present
when you're still living in the past?

Comfort Zones, Fear, and Emotional Avoidance

It's time to get real and vulnerable.

Most people don't avoid real estate because it's complicated.
They avoid it because they're afraid, and it's uncomfortable.

This uncomfortable feeling shows up in a thousand little ways — and it keeps us from doing the very things we must do in order to succeed:

Talking to the seller.
Asking for what you really want.
Making an offer.
Negotiating.
Raising capital.
Doing the math.
Prospecting and digging for deals.

Underneath all of it is one thing:

Fear.

Not soft fear.
Not mild fear.

A fear that's **deceptive** —
a fear that disguises itself as caution
and sometimes even as wisdom.

And you telegraph that fear to others whether you realize it or not.

Fear says:

"Let's wait."
"They may not like us."
"What if I make a mistake?"
"What if something goes wrong?"
"What if I actually get the deal… then what?"

Fear protects your comfort zone…

but the comfort zone is the silent killer of potential.

Here's a fact most people never understand:

Fear blocks your dreams. Faith opens them.

When fear is driving, you hesitate.
When faith is driving, you act.

Faith isn't religious.
It's vision.
It's courage.
It's possibility.
It's seeing beyond what your fear is trying to protect.

The Imposter: Identity and Self-Esteem

It's time to get real and look in the mirror.

You can know the strategies…
You can work your tail off…
You can have big dreams…

Then the voice starts whispering:

"I'm not the kind of person who deserves success."
"It works for them, but not for me."
"What happens when they find out I'm a fraud?"
"Why do I always jump in over my head?"
"What's wrong with me? Why do I feel this way?"

That voice is the Imposter.

And that Imposter is mean —
a bully that punches you in the gut
and rips out your confidence.

It doesn't attack your goals —
it attacks your **identity.**

Because if your identity says:

"I'm not good enough."
"I'm not worthy."
"I'm not ready."
"I'm not valuable."
"I'm not lovable."

…then your actions will follow that identity every single time.

This is why people sabotage themselves right when they're about to break through.

Deep down, their inner identity isn't aligned with success yet.

And that's exactly why we need to rewrite the script —
and start loving ourselves instead of beating ourselves up.

To be successful, you **must** learn how to love yourself better.

It's not hard to rewrite the script.
Just start saying these phrases with intention and purpose —
preferably while looking into a mirror, eye to eye,
so the message goes deeper:

"I'm sorry."
"Please forgive me."

"I love you."
"Thank you."

Repeat them until you start believing them.
Once you believe them, you can add other affirmations like:

"I am worthy."
"I deserve success."
"I make the world a better place."
"I am needed and loved."

We're not talking about mushy, romantic love here.
We're talking about the kind of self-love that starts within and expands outward.

Love is presence.
Love is identity.
Love is choosing yourself.

It's the emotional anchor that aligns your life.

How to Break Through Your Internal Ceiling

Everything we just talked about —
your beliefs,
your fear,
your identity…

These things form your **internal ceiling.**

And here's the good news:

A ceiling is not a wall.

It's meant to be broken.

Your internal ceiling was built from:

- limiting beliefs
- fear
- past stories
- present identity
- old experiences
- the pain we carry

None of these reflect who you are now
or where you're meant to go.

When you start shifting your inside…
your outside automatically follows.

We'll dive further into this in the next chapter,
when we explore the full **FFL Modality**:

Faith expands your future.
Forgiveness frees your past.
Love strengthens your present.

When those three align,
there is no ceiling —
because the sky becomes your limit.

This is where real momentum begins.

Summary

So let's bring this together:

Most people get stuck because:

- their beliefs don't match their goals
- fear disguises itself as caution
- their identity doesn't allow growth
- and they sabotage themselves without realizing it

You're not stuck because you're weak.
You're stuck because you've been operating under old programming.

The next question becomes:

How do we rewrite that programming? How do we align your past, present, and future so they work with you instead of against you? How do we build the operating system that creates courage, clarity, and consistency?

That's exactly what Chapter 3 is all about.

It's time to move forward into the **FFL Wealth System.**

CHAPTER 3
THE FFL WEALTH SYSTEM™

Most people think success comes from tactics — strategies, formulas, scripts, systems. And yeah, you absolutely need the mechanics. However, even with all the right tools, you still won't get what you're looking for if you're off.

It's like a carpenter who has the best hammer and nails in the world — if he's off, he's going to hit his thumb.

Everything you've read up to this point has been preparation for who we are right now.

Because behind every stalled dream, every abandoned goal, every half-finished plan…
is an operating system running in the background that's sabotaging the front end.

It's kind of like owning a sandwich shop where one of your trusted employees is shaving a little ham off the bone for himself. On the outside, it looks like everything's fine, but inside you can feel something's off. When you don't know — you don't know.
Once you DO know, you can't un-know it.

So first things first—let's get that house in order.

You can't build wealth on top of instability.
You can't build confidence on top of guilt.
You can't build decisions on top of fear.

You can't build a new life on top of an old identity.

If your inner world isn't in order, how can your outer world ever thrive?

That's where the FFL Wealth System comes in —
Faith, Forgiveness, and Love.

This is the system I developed out of necessity — setbacks, losses, rebuilding, transformation. Not from a textbook. Not from theory. From LIFE.

Life happened. I lost. I rebuilt.
And I learned how to get recentered again and again.

The FFL Wealth System isn't personal-development fluff.
It's a **battle-tested wealth framework** that strengthens the only real asset you carry into every deal:

YOU.

Let's break down the system that will rewrite your future.

Faith: Your Future Self and Vision

Faith isn't about religion.
It's not dogma.
It's not ritual.

Faith is vision.

Faith is the ability to see something before it exists.
Faith is the courage to take a step without all the answers.

Faith is acting on a possibility that fear says you're not ready for.

Faith is the voice that says:

"I got this."
"Everything's going to be all right."
"Life is good, and I am blessed."

Faith is the fuel behind every forward-moving decision.

Without faith, every step feels terrifying.
With faith, the path might still feel scary — you just walk it anyway.

Faith expands your future by shifting what you see when you look ahead.

When people fail to take action in real estate, it's rarely because of the spreadsheets.
It's because their **vision is capped.**

Their future is too small.
Their imagination is too limited.
Their identity is too short-sighted.

Faith opens the view.

Faith lets you see deals where others don't.
Faith sees opportunity where others only see problems.
Faith allows you to see your future self — confident, capable, competent — even when today's version feels unsure.

Faith gives you the ability to manifest:

the right deals,
the right investors,
the right opportunities,
the right momentum,
and the wealthy life you deserve.

Faith enlarges your internal lens so you can grow into it.

Forgiveness: Releasing Past Challenges and Emotional Weight

If faith is for the future,
forgiveness is for the past.

And this one is heavy for most people because forgiveness requires honesty — not excuses.

Forgiveness releases the emotional weight that keeps you from moving.

It's the guilt you still carry.
It's the regret from mistakes you haven't healed from.
It's the shame from choices you made when you thought you knew better.
It's the "Why did I…?" and "I should have…" that loop in your head and drain your energy.

You can't walk very far if you're carrying boulders from the past.

Forgiveness is the tool that cuts those chains.

Forgiveness isn't about forgetting the past — you need those lessons.

It's about letting go of the emotional poison so the past doesn't own you anymore.

It's not denying pain.
It's walking through it…
and letting it go.

And yes — forgiveness is also essential in real estate.

Because we WILL make mistakes.

I know this personally.

When the 2008 financial crisis hit, I owned 30 homes.
I lost everything.
I filed bankruptcy for $4.5 million.
Lost the home I lived in.
I had three kids and a father-in-law with dementia to care for.

I felt the pain.
I lived the regret.
I know remorse intimately.

Forgiveness saved my life.

Forgiveness says:

"It's time to cut it loose. Learn from it. Move on."

Blaming people, places, and things won't fix anything — that's victim mentality.
Forgiveness is **solution mentality.**

And the hardest person to forgive is always the same:
the one in the mirror.

Until you forgive yourself,
your present stays haunted
and your future stays limited.

When you take responsibility for your actions, something powerful happens:

Your subconscious shifts from "victim"…
to the **creator** of your story.

Release the old energy so you can create new wealth.

Love: Alignment, Integrity, and Present-Moment Action

If faith guides the future
and forgiveness frees the past…

Love grounds you in the **present.**

Not romance.
Not mushy stuff.
Not greeting-card love.

Love is:

alignment.
integrity.
gratitude.
self-worth.
presence.

Love is the energy you bring into a room.
Love is the identity you carry.
Love is the compassion that keeps you centered so you can take action.

Most people think wealth comes from aggression or domination.
The truth?

Real wealth is relationship-based.
And real relationships are built on love-based presence — not fear-based pressure.

Love gives you:

- emotional clarity
- grounded decision-making
- authentic connection
- real trust from partners
- confidence without ego
- stability during uncertainty

Love is the "NOW" energy.

You can't negotiate well if you're angry or greedy.
You can't underwrite properly if you're scared.
You can't raise capital if you're insecure.
How can people believe in you if you don't?

It's even hard to sleep at night when you don't love the man in the mirror.

Love centers you.
Love aligns you with your highest self, not your scared self.

Love lets you treat people (and yourself) with integrity and respect.

This is the energy wealth responds to.

And since we're talking about love, here's the truth:

Gratitude is an expression of love.

You pay your mortgage because you're grateful to have a home.
You make your car payment because you're grateful to drive.
You donate because you're grateful to help others.

The way you spend money is simply a mirror of what you love.

The FFL Wealth System: The Missing Framework the Gurus Don't Teach

You can take a hundred courses.
You can master every formula.
Learn every strategy.
Understand every negotiation tactic.

But if your:

vision is small
past is heavy
identity is fractured

…then none of the mechanics will matter.

The FFL Wealth System:

- expands your future (Faith)
- frees your past (Forgiveness)

- aligns your present (Love)

This is the internal architecture real wealth is built on.

Every deal, every negotiation, every partnership, every decision…

is filtered through your internal system.

When FFL is active:

You see opportunities earlier.
You recognize value faster.
You recover from setbacks easier.
You negotiate with integrity.
You attract better relationships.
You make cleaner decisions.
You stay grounded under pressure.
You grow sustainably.
You feel better about who you are.
You become a leader people trust.

This is what the gurus never teach —

Because they focus on tactics, not transformation.
Mechanics, not mindset.
Spreadsheets, not self-alignment.

FFL is the piece they're missing.

Once you integrate it, everything else gets easier.

Summary

Let's bring this home:

Faith opens your future and expands your vision.
Forgiveness releases the shame, guilt, and regret from your past.
Love grounds your present and aligns your identity.

Together, these three form **The FFL Wealth System** —
the internal structure that lets every strategy in this book flow like a river of wealth.

Real estate doesn't respond to fear, insecurity, or past trauma.
It responds to alignment, confidence, clarity, and energy.

The next question becomes:

How do we apply these principles to REAL real estate?
How do we turn inner alignment into profitable decisions?
How do we merge neuroscience with strategy in a way that attracts wealth?

Now we move into **PART II — The Internal Renovation**.

PART II

THE INTERNAL RENOVATION

BECOMING WEALTHY

CHAPTER 4
FAITH: SEEING VALUE, ENHANCING VISION

Faith is the first pillar for a reason.

Not because it sounds pretty.
Not because it's poetic.
Not because it fits neatly inside a three-letter acronym.

Faith comes first because everything in your life — and everything in real estate — begins with what you can **believe** in your mind, even if you don't see it with your eyes… yet.

Faith is vision.
Faith is clarity.
Faith is energy.
Faith is that internal light that shines on your path before your feet ever touch the ground.

Most people don't fail because they're weak.
They fail because their vision is limited — limited by fear, by "what ifs," by distractions, by self-doubt.

If you can't see yourself winning, you won't.
If you can't see the deal working, it won't.
If you can't imagine what that house might become, then it never will.
And if you can't see your own worth… none of this matters.

This chapter is about strengthening the eyes of your future so you can move with confidence in the present — toward something real, something powerful, something **you create.**

So ask yourself one simple question:

How can I build the future I want… if I can't visualize what I want it to look like?

Recognizing Your Own Worth First

Let's get brutally honest:

Most people struggle with faith not because they lack belief in God, the universe, or possibility…

They struggle because they don't believe in themselves.

I've said this in my social media reels more times than I can count:

"You're the maker of your own destiny."
"You are stronger than you realize."
"You're capable of achieving anything you set your mind to."
"You got this."

Faith starts with seeing value internally — not externally.

Because if you don't see your worth:

- you will under-offer
- you will over-explain
- you will apologize for things you aren't responsible for
- you will jump into the wrong deals
- you will partner with the wrong people
- you will negotiate from fear
- you will back away when opportunity arrives

And the universe does not expand opportunities for people who silently sabotage themselves.

Faith is the part of you that says:

"I am chosen for this. I am called to this. I am built for this."

Even when the past tries to interrupt your present.
Even when doubt whispers its lies.
Even when you feel under-qualified, underprepared, or not good enough.

Faith is the identity that steps forward even when certainty hasn't shown up yet.

You attract opportunities that match your identity.

So here's a principle that needs to be engraved into your mindset:

"When you see your own value and deeply believe in yourself, you can trust yourself — and the world adjusts accordingly."

Visualization, Future Pacing, and Manifestation

Visualization is NOT daydreaming.
Future pacing is NOT pretending.
Manifestation is NOT magic.

These are **neuroscientific tools** that train your brain to recognize and pursue opportunity.

The mind does not move toward confusion.
The mind moves toward clarity.

When you visualize something repeatedly:

- your reticular activation system (RAS) turns on
- your subconscious searches for evidence
- you begin seeing proof everywhere
- your actions align with what you imagine
- your emotions sync with your direction
- your identity shifts into a person who naturally carries faith

That's why the most successful people — athletes, CEOs, entertainers, leaders — all use visualization.

Your brain rehearses success before your body ever achieves it.

And faith is the energy behind that rehearsal.

Faith says:

"I see it. I feel it. I know it. I believe it. And I'm moving toward it."

Future pacing places your mind where your feet have not stepped yet.
Manifestation aligns your energy with the life you're building.

This isn't wishful thinking.

This is neuroscience.

When you act in alignment with your true identity, your destiny begins bending toward you.

Recognizing Value Outside Yourself

Real estate mirrors a deeper truth:

Value is not always visible at first glance.

A rundown duplex…
A tired landlord…
A deferred-maintenance property…
A seller who's drowning in life…
A listing everyone else ignores…

Most people see issues.

Faith sees opportunity.

Because faith teaches you to look past:

- graffiti
- broken drywall
- overgrown landscaping
- late-paying tenants
- cosmetic damage

Faith sees what can be — not just what is.

But here's something people get wrong:

Most think hope, faith, and trust are the same thing.

They're not.

Hope is like buying a lottery ticket — you want it to happen, but you're unsure.
Hope is a shadow of faith.

Faith is the belief — the inner knowing that something is possible even before the evidence appears.

Trust is when you act on that faith.

Let me give you an example.

When my son was two years old, I placed him on top of the refrigerator and said:

"Jump into Daddy's arms."

At first, he hoped I'd catch him.
Then he started to believe I would.
But the moment his feet left the fridge—when he went airborne—that was **trust.**

Faith creates vision.
Trust creates movement.

People with faith say:

"I'm going to turn this into something beautiful."

That's what makes you a visionary.
That's what makes you a creator.
That's what makes you an investor instead of a spectator.

Because here's the truth:

"Faith doesn't ignore reality — it expands it."

Faith Opens Your Eyes to Opportunities Others Miss

Faith widens your field of possibility.

It is the ingredient that lets you trust yourself enough to **act.**

Most people only see what's directly in front of them.

Faith lets you see:

- the deal behind the deal
- the partnership behind the introduction
- the potential behind the problem
- the opportunity behind the obstacle
- the money behind the conversation
- the transformation behind the pain

Faith is the difference between:

"I hope something happens…"
and
"I know something is on its way."

Faith is not passive.
Faith is not weak.
Faith is not fragile.

Faith is bold.
Faith creates trust.
Trust takes action.
Trust leaps forward first.
Trust moves with confidence long before certainty shows up.

So believe in yourself.
Look deep inside.
Because what you're looking for is probably in a place you haven't searched yet.

Faith lives inside you.

Faith opens doors.
Faith creates alignment.
Faith calls in opportunities.
Faith builds momentum.

Faith is the first part of the FFL Wealth System because it expands your capacity, clears your vision, and prepares your identity to receive abundance.

Summary

Faith is not a feeling.
Faith is not luck.
Faith is not a wish.

Faith is:

- your vision
- your identity in motion
- your belief in yourself
- your ability to see the deal before it exists
- your courage to step into something bigger than your past

Faith lights the road ahead.

It opens your eyes to opportunities others miss.
It activates your potential.
It expands your identity.
It aligns you with abundance.
It elevates you into the version of yourself that wins.

And now that we've strengthened your ability to trust yourself and trust the path,
it's time to address the emotional weight that keeps most people stuck.

You cannot step into your future while dragging yesterday in your pocket.

And that's exactly what the next chapter is about.

Let's move forward into Chapter 5 — Forgiveness: Clearing Past Challenges & Opening the Door to Freedom.

CHAPTER 5

FORGIVENESS: CLEARING PAST PAIN & OPENING THE DOOR TO FREEDOM

Forgiveness is one of the most misunderstood forces in human transformation.

People think forgiveness is about changing how you feel.
It's not.

Forgiveness is about changing your mindset.
Forgiveness is about changing your identity.
Forgiveness is about freeing your present from your past.

Because you cannot become the person you're destined to be
if you're still chained to the person you've always been.

If Faith removes fear so you can live in the present,
then Forgiveness removes the past so you can stay in the present.

And the present is where life actually happens.
Time is precious.
Time is the only currency we spend without knowing how much we have left.

Yesterday is a canceled check.
Tomorrow is a promissory note.
Today is cash in hand.

And cash in hand is all that counts —
because the time is always now.

The present is a gift —
that's why they call it the present.

Forgiveness becomes the bridge that carries you from who you were…
into who you are right now.

And trust me…
I know it ain't easy.
I've had to forgive — then redefine myself — more times than I can count.

Understanding How Our Past Binds Us

Beliefs build behavior.
Behavior builds patterns.
Patterns build identity.

Negative behavior patterns lead to pain…
pain leads to wounds…
and if we don't heal those wounds, they turn into scars.

Scars may be permanent —
they do not have to dictate your destiny.

You cannot let the past define who you are.
That victim mentality will never lead to freedom.

Every one of us carries emotional debris —

little twigs, old leaves, tiny pieces of broken memories
that drift into the mind and gather in the corners.

I call this **the muck.**

The muck clogs the river of success —
the flow toward wealth, clarity, connection, and opportunity.

And it's not always the "big stuff" that blocks the flow.

Most of the time it's the little things that accumulate:

old beliefs
childhood wounds
shame behind behavior
regret from bad choices
guilt we never addressed
things that happened — or didn't happen —
real or imagined

One piece at a time, even when it feels small…
over time it becomes a massive pile of emotional rubbish
that jams the flow completely.

First the river slows.
Then it weakens.
Then it stops altogether —
becoming a stagnant puddle of negativity and excuses.

Forgiveness is the process of clearing the muck —
sometimes twig by twig…
sometimes breaking apart a whole cluster at once.

Forgiveness is not forgetting the past.
Forgiveness is learning from the past,
taking the lesson with you,
and letting the pain go so it stops choking your present.

Because how can you live in today
if your mind is still reliving yesterday?

Releasing Regret, Guilt, and Emotional Clutter

Most people think they're stuck because of circumstances.
They blame people, places, things, or events.

They don't realize the real blockage is internal —
a dam built inside their mind and reinforced by their emotions.

Regret.
Shame.
Self-blame.
Guilt.
Remorse.
Unresolved pain.

Old self-defeating beliefs.

This emotional clutter becomes a belief system —
a belief system made of hurt, blame, and fear.

And the more you replay those old tapes,
the more debris you throw onto the dam.

Even traditional "talk therapy" can backfire.
People say, "Talk it out…"
yet if all you do is relive it,
you're not talking it out —
you're talking it in.

You're reliving those emotions over and over again, deepening them.

Negativity invites more negativity.
Fear breeds more fear.
Pain attracts more pain.

Soon the subconscious begins whispering:

"Here we go again…"
"You always mess things up."
"You can't trust yourself."
"You're no good."
"You don't deserve anything better."
"People like you never catch a break."

That's the voice of the dam.
That's the sound of the muck piling up.

Forgiveness is the only force that cuts through that debris.

Forgiveness says:

"It happened… yet it does not define me."
"I accept the past, learn from it, and release its chains."
"I accept myself as human."
"I'm willing to take responsibility, make amends, and clear the wreckage of my past."
"I am free from the pain that used to bind me."

Because until you release the emotional clutter:

you can't see clearly
you can't decide clearly
you can't trust yourself fully

You can't walk into today
carrying yesterday's pain on your back.

How Forgiveness Breaks the Chains That Bind Us

Forgiveness is not just emotional.
Forgiveness is **action.**

And that action is called **amends.**

Amends is not simply saying "I'm sorry."
Amends is responsibility.
Amends is cleaning your side of the street.
Amends is correcting the behavior
so you don't repeat it again.

There are three kinds of amends:

- **Direct amends** — repairing something directly with another person
- **Indirect amends** — when you can't repair it directly
- **Self-amends** — the most important one of all

Self-amends means:

stop beating yourself up and put down the whip
identify your assets and grow them
break the patterns that have blocked you
let go of the vices you keep secret
be grateful for who you are
treat yourself better
care for your body and your mind because you deserve it
eat healthier
rest when needed
meditate
exercise
live intentionally

Self-amends is being grateful for who you are.
It is an act of love.

Forgiveness without amends is incomplete.
It's like pulling the weeds and leaving the roots —
you're never fully free from the problem.

And here's a personal story of forgiveness that changed my life forever…

I carried the weight of my father's death for decades.

He died when I was eleven —
young, addicted, hurting, drowning in his own life.

For years, I carried wounds that hardened into beliefs:

"Why did my dad leave us?"
"Wasn't I good enough?"
"Why can't I cry more?"
"What's wrong with me?"

I carried that pain into everything —
sports, relationships, work, addiction, success.

Nothing released it.
Nothing unclogged the river.

Until one day in Cumberland, Maryland… in the rain…
I saw a single flower growing in the forest.

Something inside me whispered,
"That flower is for your dad."

I picked it.
Drove to the cemetery.
Walked through the rain.
Knelt at his headstone.

He died at 35.
And in that moment… I realized I was 35.

And I had a son around the same age I was when he overdosed.

I realized something deeper:

The cycle had broken.

I was clean.
Clear-minded.
Present.
Alive.

No longer the addict I once was.

And in that moment — standing in the rain, holding a flower —
I saw him differently… as a human.

Nothing he had done changed.
My perspective changed.
And I changed.

Not because I tried harder.
Not because I forced it.
Not because time healed it.

Because the process of forgiveness had begun.

My mindset shifted.
My attitude softened.
My identity opened.

I removed the label of "Dad" from him.
And when I removed that label,
I removed all the expectations I had placed on him.

I saw him as an addict —
a human prone to mistakes —
a man who let himself down long before he let me down.

A man drowning in pain.
A man full of regret and remorse.
A man who didn't know how to cope.
A man who probably thought we were better off without him.

Suddenly, resentment cracked.
Judgment melted.
Pain dissolved.

And for the first time in my life,
I felt empathy and compassion.

I know in my heart that my dad loved me,
and I loved him.

Forgiveness didn't erase the memory —
forgiveness rewrote the story.

And standing there in the rain…
the dam broke.
And I broke.
I cried relentlessly.
I was no longer the same.

Flow returned.
Identity shifted.
I was free.

The Path to Acceptance and New Possibilities

Forgiveness is a process —
a clearing, a cleansing,
a transformation of mind and spirit.

There are **three things** I learned that day in the rain:

1. **You can't live in today if you're still reliving yesterday.**
2. **Forgiveness takes work — amends, emotional, mental, and spiritual.**
3. **Forgiveness creates freedom — the kind that opens the door to possibility.**

When forgiveness happens:

clarity returns
peace returns
creativity opens
self-worth rises
identity strengthens
momentum awakens
your dreams finally become possible

Forgiveness doesn't change the past.
Forgiveness changes you —
so the past no longer owns you.

Forgiveness moves you
from being a victim
to becoming an active participant in your life again.

Summary

Let's bring it all home:

- The muck becomes an emotional dam over time.
- Amends — with others, the world, and yourself — is the tool that clears it.
- Forgiveness removes the debris and restores flow.
- Forgiveness is the key that unlocks the door to freedom.
- Your past does not define who you are — it guides you toward who you choose to be.

The obvious next question is…

What do you want your present to look like? How do you stay grounded? Now that fear and the muck are gone — how do we deal with our selfish nature?

Well… are you ready for Love?

Because that's where we're headed in **Chapter 6—Love: Making Dreams a Reality.**

CHAPTER 6
LOVE: MAKING DREAMS A REALITY

Love is the most powerful force in the world.

Not the romantic version.
Not the Hallmark version.
Not the soft, sugar-coated version.

Love — real love — is the energy of alignment, integrity, service, connection, presence, and truth.

Love is the principle that makes dreams a reality.

Just like fear, anxiety, and worry distort the future…
and regret, shame, and guilt distort the past…

Those selfish tendencies — anger, greed, jealousy, resentment, ego — distort the present.

And the present is the only place where life actually happens.

Love is the principle that keeps you anchored in the now.

Love is mindfulness.
Love is awareness.
Love is purpose.
Love is service.
Love is gratitude.

Love is wisdom.
Love is connection.

Love is the energy that stabilizes your internal world so everything external can flourish.

Love is the glue that binds relationships, opportunities, partnerships, and abundance together.

Love is the frequency wealth responds to.

The Foundation of All Wealth

This might be the most important sentence in the entire book:

You can't give away what you don't have.

You can't give confidence
if you don't feel confident.

You can't give compassion
if you never offer it to yourself.

You can't give respect
if you're constantly talking down to yourself.

You can't create harmony
when there's a war happening inside your head.

You can't build healthy relationships
when your relationship with yourself is wounded.

You can't sell what you offer
if you don't have the faith to invest in it yourself.

Loving yourself isn't selfish.
Loving yourself is survival.

Loving yourself connects you to that divine inner strength that lives in you.

Loving yourself is the foundation of influence, connection, and abundance.

Loving yourself sounds like:

"I matter."
"I am worthy."
"I deserve good things."
"I have value."
"I treat myself with respect."
"I will care for myself — body, mind, and spirit."

When you honor yourself the right way…

- You surround yourself with people who are healthy for you.
- You negotiate from strength and faith in your own abilities.
- You speak with clarity.
- You trust your intuition and follow your gut.
- You complete what you start.
- You break the cycle of self-sabotage.
- You make decisions from wisdom, not wounds.

Loving yourself connects you to that inner voice —
the source of personal power.

When you are aligned with that voice, miracles happen,
and transformation becomes natural.

The FFL Way of Rewriting the Heart

Forgiveness cleared the river.
Love keeps the river flowing.

Now we bring in one of the most powerful tools for emotional healing — one that transforms the inner world quickly, intensely, and deeply:

Ho'oponopono.

Here's how you do it:

Go to a mirror.
Look into your own eyes.
Let the eyes in the mirror meet the eyes in your head —
because the eyes are the window to the soul.

Then speak, out loud, with intention and purpose:

"I'm sorry."
"Please forgive me."
"I love you."
"Thank you."

Say it again.
And again.
Until you feel the shift.
Until it becomes real.

This exercise:

- heals old wounds

- dissolves self-judgment
- rewires identity
- restores worthiness
- anchors you in presence
- activates compassion
- removes shame
- strengthens self-respect

This is Love in action.
This is Love as transformation.
This is Love as energy —
the kind that changes you from the inside out.

Love Speaks Through Service

Zig Ziglar said:

"You can get everything you want in life by helping enough other people get what they want."

That is Love.

Love is service.
Love is contribution.
Love solves problems.
Love listens.
Love pays attention.
Love creates win-win situations.
Love elevates people around you.

In real estate — and in life — Love shows up through integrity.

A lot of people misunderstand that word.
They think integrity is the same as honesty.

It's not.

An honest man may confess,
"I slept with your wife."

A man of integrity
would never sleep with her in the first place.

Be known for your integrity.

Love also expresses itself through:

- compassion
- empathy
- ethical decision-making
- transparency
- creativity
- understanding others' needs
- solving others' problems
- caring about people more than transactions

Love is the currency of trust. And trust is the currency of wealth.

People follow Love.
People invest in Love.
Pcoplc partner with Love.
People return to Love.
People stay loyal to Love.

Because Love is the one energy that never deceives.

The Flow of Money

We talked earlier about money as energy.

Now let's take it deeper:

Money flows toward Love because Love flows through gratitude.

Every time you spend money,
you're expressing appreciation:

You pay your mortgage because you're grateful for the home.
You buy food because you're grateful to be nourished.
You pay your car payment because you're grateful for the transportation.
You donate because you're grateful that you can help.
You invest because you're grateful for opportunity.

Gratitude is Love in motion.

Love transcends the Law of Manifestation
because when money is aligned with Love and gratitude…

…it flows through:

The Law of Reciprocity

— service given in Love returns multiplied.

The Law of Affinity

— wealth expands where appreciation grows.

Before we move forward, let's make this crystal clear:

Gratitude is not a feeling. Gratitude is an action.

Let me tell you a quick story:

When my older son was 16, we bought him a blue Datsun — a stick shift.
He was not grateful for that Datsun.
He never washed it.
Never changed the oil.
Barely cared for it.
I think I remember it catching fire in the K-Mart parking lot.

A few years later he bought his own car — a red automatic sports car.
He loved that car.
Washed it constantly.
Kept it spotless.

He appreciated it.

That's gratitude.
Not lip service. Action

Love isn't forcing.
Love isn't demanding.
Love isn't controlling.

Love is allowing.
Love is trusting.
Love is appreciating.
Love is actively participating in the flow of life.

Real estate responds to Love because Love brings:

- clarity
- calm
- intuition
- connection
- generosity
- confidence
- courage
- authenticity

These are the energies that make deals happen.
These are the energies investors trust.
These are the energies that build long-term wealth.

Love Strengthens All Relationships

Love is the glue of human connection.

Whether it's:

- a partner
- an investor
- a seller
- a buyer
- a tenant
- a spouse
- a colleague
- a child
- a friend

Love is what strengthens the bond.

Love is attentiveness.
Love is understanding.
Love is listening.
Love is patience.
Love is presence.
Love is compassion without weakness.
Love is strength without ego.

Love is the highest form of communication — beyond words.

Because people remember how you made them **feel**.

And when people feel safe, seen, heard, valued, and respected…

They stay.
They follow.
They trust.
They open doors.
They recommend you.
They work with you.
They stay connected to you.

Love is the energy that builds networks, communities, partnerships, investors, and lifelong relationships.

Love is influence — the right kind.
Love is impact — the lasting kind.

The Ripple Effect

Love doesn't stop with you.

When you act from Love,
you create ripple effects that reach:

- rooms you haven't entered
- opportunities you didn't know existed
- people you've never met
- moments you'll never see
- blessings you didn't expect

Love multiplies.

Love travels through conversations, gestures, tones, decisions, intentions, and energy.

One act of Love — a smile, a kind word, a patient moment, a helpful gesture — can change the direction of someone's day…

…which changes their decisions…
…which changes their life…
…which eventually circles back and elevates your own.

This is why Love is powerful.

Love is exponential.
Love is contagious.
Love is the principle that makes dreams a reality.

Summary

Let's tie it all together:

- Love anchors you in the present — the only place life happens.
- Love stabilizes your emotions so fear and regret lose their grip.
- Love begins with self-love — because you can't give what you don't have.

- Love expresses itself through integrity, gratitude, and service.
- Love fuels the laws of affinity and reciprocity — creating abundance.
- Love strengthens relationships and builds trust.
- Love creates ripple effects that expand opportunities in every direction.
- Love transforms your life — and your wealth.

Love is not weakness.
Love is not softness.
Love is not passive.

Love is strength.
Love is clarity.
Love is alignment.
Love is influence.
Love is truth.
Love is power.

Love is the energy that turns potential into reality.

Now that we've anchored the present — the place where life truly happens —
it's time to take all three pillars of Faith, Forgiveness, and Love…

In essence, they are the three sides of the FFL pyramid of self.
Self-worth is the base.
Divine connection is the point at the top.
The more you have faith, forgive, and love,
the wider your self-worth grows
and the higher your connection rises.

Now that your inner world is aligned…

it's time to move to the mechanics —
the math, the strategy, the action steps.

Let's move into Part III — The External Framework. This section focuses on 'Real Life Real Estate Skills'. We'll start with Chapter 7 – Know the Math & Talk the Talk.

PART III

THE EXTERNAL FRAMEWORK

REAL-LIFE REAL ESTATE SKILLS

CHAPTER 7
KNOW THE MATH & TALK THE TALK

If you want to build real wealth in real estate... If you want investors to trust you... If you want brokers, lenders, contractors, partners, and sellers to take you seriously...

Then you must know the math — and you must talk the talk.

This chapter is the foundation of everything that comes after it.

Because money follows clarity...
Wealth follows confidence...
And confidence comes from understanding the numbers and speaking the language of investors.

When you know this material cold, you can walk into any room, any negotiation, any meeting — and instantly be seen as someone who belongs at the table.

Let's get into it.

The Math

In real estate, the numbers don't lie.

They tell you whether a deal is worth pursuing, worth funding, or worth walking away from.

If you don't understand the math, you're gambling.
If you do understand the math, you're investing.

Below are the core calculations every investor must master.

Net Operating Income (NOI)

NOI is the heartbeat of any rental property.

NOI = Gross Rental Income – Operating Expenses

NOI does not include:

- Mortgage payments
- Depreciation
- Income taxes
- Capital expenditures (CapEx – major repairs)

Why NOI Matters:

- It determines the property's value in income-producing real estate
- Lenders use it
- Underwriters rely on it
- Investors make decisions from it

If you don't know NOI, you can't evaluate a rental deal.

Cap Rate

The cap rate tells you the return a property would produce if you bought it all cash.

Cap Rate = NOI ÷ Purchase Price

Examples:
NOI $50,000 ÷ $500,000 purchase = **10% cap**

NOI $50,000 ÷ $1,000,000 purchase = **5% cap**

Why Cap Rate Matters:

- It tells you risk vs reward
- Lower cap = safer, more competition
- Higher cap = more risk, more upside

General Guidelines:

- Beginners: aim for **7–12%**
- Seasoned investors: may accept lower caps for long-term appreciation

Cap rate is the first filter — not the final one.

Cash-on-Cash Return (CoC)

This tells you your return on the actual money you invested.

CoC = Annual Cash Flow ÷ Cash Invested

Example:
You invest $40,000 (down payment + closing costs)
You earn $6,000/year cash flow

CoC = 6,000 ÷ 40,000 = **15%**

A strong CoC is usually **10–20%+**.

Vacancy Rate

Vacancy rate = how often units sit empty.

It impacts:

- NOI
- Cash flow
- DSCR
- Property value

High vacancy can be a **warning sign** — or an **opportunity** (mismanagement, high rents, poor marketing).

Smart investors always dig deeper.

Loss to Lease

Difference between market rent and actual rent.

Market: $1,500
Tenant: $1,200
Loss to lease = $300/month

High loss-to-lease means:

- Lazy management
- Built-in upside
- Opportunity to reposition rents

Investors love value that can be unlocked.

The Cost of Money: DSCR, Private Money & Hard Money

Every loan has a cost — and that cost determines if the deal works.

DSCR Loans

DSCR = NOI ÷ Annual Debt Payments

Most lenders require:
1.25 DSCR or better

If DSCR is too low, the lender won't fund the deal.

DSCR loans often have:

- Lower points
- Lower interest
- Lower fees

But many properties do **not** qualify due to condition or vacancy.

That's where private or hard money steps in.

Private Money & Hard Money

These lenders care more about the **asset** than your income.

Hard money is:

- Fast
- Flexible
- Expensive

And **great for flips and assignments**.

Higher:

- Points
- Interest

- Shorter terms

But expensive money is not a problem when the profit is big.

If a $10,000 loan fee helps you secure a $150,000 profit?

That's not a cost—
That's leverage.

Total Project Cost & Flip Profit Formula

Not every deal is based on NOI.
Some deals are flips, wholetails, or value-add projects where the real question is simple:

"What's the total all-in cost, and what's the actual profit?"

Here's the formula seasoned investors use:

Total Project Cost =

**Purchase Price

- Repair/Rehab Cost
- Closing Costs (buying)
- Holding Costs
- Closing Costs (selling, including commissions & escrow fees)**

Only AFTER you know the true total cost can you calculate real profit:

Profit = ARV – Total Project Cost

Where **ARV** means **After Repair Value** — the expected market value once the work is done.

Why this matters:

- Many new investors forget holding costs.
- Many forget selling costs (commissions can eat 5–6%).
- Many underestimate rehab.
- Many ignore taxes, insurance, utilities, or loan interest during the project.

The deal isn't what you THINK you'll make.
The deal is what's left after every dollar is counted.

If you get this wrong, you lose money.
If you get this right, you print money.

Experienced investors run this calculation **before anything else** — and they walk away from any deal where the numbers don't leave enough spread to justify the risk.

Example flip math:

Purchase price: $240,000
Rehab: $45,000
Holding costs: $6,000
Closing cost buy side: $3,500
Closing cost sell side: $17,000
ARV: $360,000

Total cost: $240k + 45k + 6k + 3.5k + 17k = **$311,500**
Profit: $360,000 – $311,500 = **$48,500**

THIS is the real number.

Not the fantasy number rookies cling to.

Repairs, CapEx & Deferred Maintenance

CapEx = big-ticket, non-recurring costs:

- Roof
- HVAC
- Electrical
- Windows
- Plumbing
- Foundation

Deferred maintenance = repairs the seller ignored.

Ignore these…
And a "good deal" becomes a disaster.

Must Know Terms and Timelines

Knowing the math is essential.
Knowing the **language** makes you credible.

Purchase and Sale Agreement (PSA)

The PSA becomes binding when:

- Both parties sign
- **Consideration** is exchanged (EMD or another asset)

It is the blueprint of the entire deal.

Earnest Money Deposit (EMD)

Shows seriousness.
Held in escrow.
At risk after due diligence.

Consideration may include:

- Cash
- Property
- Notes
- Services

This matters in **creative financing**.

Due Diligence Period

Your window to:

- Inspect
- Verify income
- Read leases
- Check financials
- Price repairs
- Stress test the deal
- Renegotiate or exit

Do not skip this.

Title

Title = legal ownership.

A clean title = no issues.
A clouded title = problems to solve.

Clouded Title Examples:

- Unpaid child support judgments
- IRS liens
- Unresolved probate
- Contractor liens
- Boundary disputes
- Bankruptcy filings
- Forged signatures

Problems for the seller.
Opportunity for the investor.

Lis Pendens

Public notice of pending litigation involving the property.

Could be opportunity…
Or danger.

Liens

Legal claims against a property.

Examples:

- Tax liens
- Child support liens
- Mechanics' liens
- Judgment liens

A clean title is required to close.

Escrow

Neutral third party that:

- Holds funds
- Manages documents
- Ensures legality
- Records the deed

Nothing is final until recorded at the courthouse.

Loan Structures & Financing Terms

LTV — Loan-to-Value
Percentage lender will loan based on value.

ARV — After Repair Value
Expected value after improvements.

PITI
Principal, Interest, Taxes, Insurance.

Bridge Loans
Short-term financing until long-term financing is secured.

Mezzanine Loans
Secondary financing behind a senior loan.

Private Money
Individuals lending based on relationships and trust.

Hard Money
Asset-based lending — fast, flexible, expensive.

Balloon Payments
Large payoff at the end of a short-term loan.

Lender & Closing Costs
Origination, points, underwriting, escrow, title, recording fees.

Due-on-Sale Clause
Lender *may* call the loan due if ownership transfers.
Not always enforced — but you must understand it.

The Language of Wealth

These terms separate amateurs from professionals.

Pro Forma

Projected performance:

- Future income
- Future expenses
- Future NOI

If your projection doesn't make sense — the deal doesn't make sense.

Exit Strategy

Every deal needs a clear exit:

- Buy & hold
- Fix & flip
- **BRRRR (Buy, Rehab, Rent, Refinance, Repeat)**
- Assign
- Wholetail
- Cash-out refinance
- Partnership buyout

Never enter a deal blind.

Operating Agreement

For partnerships and LLCs.

It defines:

- Ownership
- Profit shares
- Decision-making
- Responsibilities
- What happens if someone exits

No operating agreement = guaranteed future conflict.

Certificate of Occupancy (CO)

Legal document allowing tenants to occupy a property.

No CO = no income.

Section 8

Government-subsidized housing program.

Pros: guaranteed rent.
Cons: inspections and compliance.

Rent Rolls & T-12s

Rent Roll shows:

- Who lives where
- What they pay
- When they pay
- Deposit amounts
- Lease terms
- Late history

T-12 shows:

- Past 12 months of income
- Operating expenses
- Repairs
- Utilities
- Management

- Irregularities
- Tenant problems

Professionals study both.
Rookies skip them — and lose money.

Comparative Evaluation Tools

CMA (Comparative Market Analysis)
Basic comps — often inaccurate.

BPO (Broker Price Opinion)
More accurate, done by a licensed agent.

Appraisal
Certified valuation — required by lenders.

Cost Approach
Value based on replacement cost.

Income Approach
Value = NOI ÷ Cap Rate
Used for commercial and multifamily.

Presenting Like an Experienced Investor

Once you know the math and the language…

You show up differently.

You negotiate differently.
You think differently.
You build differently.

You attract differently.

People feel your confidence.

And this is *exactly* why I was brought into **3D Real Estate Developers** as a partner.

It wasn't because of my money.
It wasn't because of my credit.
It was because of my:

- Knowledge
- Integrity
- Experience
- And the **energy** I carried

People want to work with someone who speaks the language, understands the math, and radiates certainty.

When you can talk the talk and walk the walk…
Doors open.
Opportunities appear.
Partnerships form.
Money finds you.

Summary

Before you can buy property…
Before you can negotiate…
Before you can raise capital…
Before you can build a team…

You must **know the math and talk the talk.**

Now you understand:

- How investors analyze deals
- How returns are measured
- How lenders evaluate risk
- How to identify value
- How to speak the language of wealth
- How to present like a pro
- How to earn trust instantly

Because of this chapter…

You're ready for the next step.

Now we move into the heart of the game:

Next Up — Negotiation Through Presence, Sensory Acuity & Communication

CHAPTER 8
NEGOTIATION THROUGH PRESENCE, SENSORY ACUITY & COMMUNICATION

Ethical Disclaimer — Read This First

The tools you're about to learn in this chapter can change lives.
They can dissolve resistance.
Shift emotions.
Create trust.
Turn confusion into clarity.
And turn two strangers into aligned partners.

These same tools, if used without integrity, can harm people, pressure people, and manipulate people into decisions that are **not in their best interest**.

So let's set the rule for this chapter — and the rule for your entire career:

"Influence is a responsibility. Use these tools ONLY to help people, not to take advantage of them."

Integrity is not optional.
Intent is everything.
Your job as a negotiator is to create alignment, not victims.

If your motives are pure…
If your aim is to be of service…
If you operate from responsibility, clarity, and truth…

Then the techniques in this chapter will make your life easier, your relationships stronger, and your success inevitable.

With that said…

Let's begin.

Identity: The Inner Script of Influence

Before any negotiation begins…
Before you talk numbers…
Before you solve challenges…
Before you make an offer…

People form an instant conclusion:

"Can I trust this person?"

Every negotiation — in real estate or in life — begins with identity, energy, and presence.

People don't follow scripts.
People don't follow spreadsheets.
People don't follow charm.

People follow conviction.
People follow confidence.
People follow alignment.
People follow YOU.

Your Energy Negotiates Before Your Words Do

Your energy is your first impression.
It communicates:

- confidence or insecurity
- clarity or confusion
- leadership or hesitation
- authenticity or insincerity
- abundance or scarcity

Before you speak, the other person's nervous system is already reading you.

This is **neuroception** — the mind scanning for:

- safety
- threat
- opportunity

If their mind perceives threat, they won't hear your logic.
If their mind perceives safety, they open to connection, collaboration, and alignment.

This is why your presence matters more than your pitch.

Self-Belief Is Contagious

If **you** don't buy you…
they won't buy you.

If you don't believe in the deal…

they won't believe in the deal.

Identity is the foundation of influence.

You are communicating:

- I know what I'm doing.
- I understand the numbers.
- I understand the market.
- I am honest.
- I am consistent.
- I solve problems.
- I follow through.

This is what makes people have faith in you.

Rapport Without Manipulation

Real rapport is NOT:

- mimicking someone like a robot
- copying gestures to "get one over on them"
- forcing connection

Real rapport is:

- matching emotional tempo
- mirroring tone naturally
- pacing their concerns
- aligning your attention with theirs
- making them feel seen, safe, and understood

Tools include:

- **sensory acuity** — reading micro-shifts in expression and posture to be aware of your effect on them
- **mirroring** — matching energy naturally, syncing together like two gears moving in harmony
- **pacing statements** — acknowledging their reality with clarity
- **leading statements** — gently guiding the conversation toward alignment

These techniques are **powerful when used together, and in the right sequence**.
Used ethically, they remove friction and build trust.
Used manipulatively, they destroy reputations.

So keep your integrity.

Identity Creates Influence

The strongest negotiators move from identity:

- calm
- aware
- grounded

- confident
- empathetic
- solution-oriented
- trustworthy
- in control of their own state

A negotiator isn't something you do.
It is something you become.

Eliminating Fear Through Understanding Challenges

In every negotiation, it is important to realize that there are no obstacles — only **challenges**.

Every challenge is a clue.
A signal.
An invitation.

People say things like:

"I need to think about it."
"I'm not sure."
"I'm nervous about X."
"I don't know if this is the right move."

These are NOT objections.
These are NOT rejections.

These are challenges — doorways into what the other person really needs.

Challenges expose:

- fear
- uncertainty
- missing information
- personal pressure
- emotional risk
- past experiences
- hidden motives
- deeper desires

A challenge is NEVER about the surface words.

Fear Is the Invisible Opponent

In every negotiation, there are always two conversations:

- the words being spoken
- the fear beneath those words

People fear:

- losing money
- making a mistake
- being taken advantage of
- not being informed
- the unknown
- embarrassment
- regret

Your job is to reduce fear, not increase it.

Safety Opens the Brain

The brain **opens** emotionally when logic is readily available.

When someone feels safe:

- emotion settles
- logic turns on
- creativity increases
- collaboration rises
- solutions appear
- trust grows
- genuine concern is felt
- alignment becomes possible

How do you create that safety?

You listen to understand, not to respond.

Most people listen with the intent to reply.
Great negotiators listen with the intent to understand.

You pace their concerns:

"You're right — that would make me nervous too."
"That makes total sense why you'd feel that way."
"I'm glad you said that — it helps me understand what matters most to you."

Pacing lowers their guard.
Lowered guard opens trust.
Open trust leads to alignment.

A challenge is not a problem.

A challenge is an opportunity to discover needs.

The Dance: Leading in Harmony

Negotiation is not combat.
Negotiation is a **dance**.

The goal is not to win.
The goal is to **align**.

Two people…
moving together…
toward a shared destination.

This is the art.

Pacing → Leading

Pacing aligns you with their perspective.
Leading guides them toward new possibilities.

Pacing:
"I understand that the timeline feels tight."

Leading:
"Let's explore how we can build in more flexibility without losing momentum."

This creates movement, not force.

Guiding Them to Their Own Conclusion

Real influence makes them feel like *they discovered* the solution.

You ask:

"What would make this feel like the right decision for you?"
"What needs to be true for you to feel confident moving forward?"
"What would a perfect outcome look like?"
"If we solved X, would Y become easier?"

People commit deeper to solutions they help create.

No, because... → Yes, if...

"No, because the repair cost scares me"
→ "Yes, if we can confirm the contractor bids and build a contingency buffer."

"No, because the timeline feels fast"
→ "Yes, if we can clarify each step of the process."

Real Estate Application

When a seller says, "I just need more time,"
they're not resisting the deal —
they're asking for **emotional safety, clarity, and alignment**.

When you pace that need
and guide them toward a solution...

the negotiation shifts from conflict to collaboration.

This is the dance in action.

Conviction + Communication = Connection

When identity, safety, and alignment merge…
negotiation becomes effortless.

Conviction Is the Ultimate Negotiation Energy

Conviction is NOT certainty.
Certainty implies promises.
Conviction implies **energy.**

Conviction is the belief in:

- your work
- your math
- your strategy
- your integrity
- your ability to find solutions
- your ability to follow through

Conviction is magnetic.
Conviction communicates leadership without arrogance.

Communication Creates Connection

Communication creates:

- partnership
- trust
- enthusiasm
- cooperation
- clarity

- shared vision

Communication is the key to alignment.
And when people feel aligned with you…

the negotiation is already won.

Connection Is the Ultimate Strategic Goal

This is what happens when you:

- have the right identity
- create emotional safety
- dance toward alignment
- move with conviction
- influence ethically

You become:

- trustworthy
- effective
- reliable
- impressive
- magnetic
- irresistible

People WANT to say yes to you because you make them feel:

- understood
- supported
- aligned
- secure
- confident

That's connection.
That's the secret.
That's negotiation mastery.

Ethical Influence Builds Empires

Manipulation destroys careers.
Integrity builds empires.

Ethical influence:

- prioritizes their needs
- respects their convictions
- honors their values
- builds long-term relationships

Your reputation is your wealth.

Summary

Now you understand:

The Identity of Influence

- Why people must trust YOU
- Why confidence and conviction matter
- How neuroception shapes first impressions
- How presence speaks louder than words

The Safety of Understanding

- Why challenges are not objections
- Why fear is the hidden enemy

- How to listen to understand
- How to pace and reframe

The Dance of Alignment

- Pacing → leading
- Guiding toward shared conclusions
- Turning resistance into cooperation
- Conversational movement toward solutions

The Ultimate Equation

Conviction + Communication = Connection

- Conviction — faith in each other
- Communication — finding common ground
- Connection — syncing alignment

The Power of Ethical Integration

- Influence with integrity
- Leadership without pressure
- Conviction without arrogance
- Alignment without manipulation

Negotiation is not about pushing.
Negotiation is not about convincing.
Negotiation is not about overpowering.

Negotiation is about:

Identity
Safety

Harmony
Connection

When you master these four elements…
every conversation becomes an opportunity for collaboration, mutual success, and connection.

And now…
You're ready for the next stage of the journey.

Next Up: Chapter 9 — Acquisitions: Seizing Control.

CHAPTER 9
ACQUISITIONS: SEIZING CONTROL

If you want to become a successful real estate investor, everything starts with acquisitions — **seizing control of the asset.**

A deal occurs the moment control of a property transfers from one party to another.
Without a deal, you don't have an opportunity.
And without the right systems to consistently find or control assets, you don't have a business.

In a nutshell, that's the flow of real estate transactions.

This chapter is not fluff.
This is real estate meat.
The Blueprint.

This is the part of the book where you learn exactly how to find real deals, solve real problems, and build a solid real estate portfolio — **with or without your own money.**

There are really only two ways to get deals:

- **Deals find you**, or
- **You find deals.**

Many people think the only way to get deals is to grind, hustle, and chase. And yes, there's a season for that. But I also know from experience that deals can and do come to you — sometimes in waves — when you become known as the person who **solves real estate problems.**

That's the **Law of Attraction** in action.

Deals come to you when people believe you're:

- That real estate guy
- The problem-solver
- The one who shows up, follows through, and finds creative solutions
- Someone they can trust

The other way is through the **Law of Manifestation** — where you see what you want, decide what you're going after, and then put in the footwork to go out there and get it.

In reality, it all comes down to two paths:

- **Deals find you.**
- **You find deals.**

Either way is powerful, and acquisition is **exponentially multiplied** when you combine those two with the **Law of Universal Influence** — where your energy, your words, and your actions create ripple effects that impact the world around you and influence your returns.

We're going to break all of this down and give you everything you need to become the kind of investor people trust.

Where the Good Deals Are

Just like there are multiple ways to find deals, there are also clear signs that help you identify **good** deals.

A **good deal** is a deal where you have a strong potential to make money and be compensated fairly for the problems you solve.
A **bad deal** is a deal where you don't get an adequate return on your investment — or you're taking on way too much risk for way too little reward.

As a general rule of thumb, good, experienced real estate investors avoid bad deals like the plague. But we're all human, and we're all subject to mistakes every now and then.

That said, it's safe to say that the **best** deals usually come from two main sources:

1. **Distressed properties**, or
2. **Distressed owners.**

Scenarios like these open the door for opportunity **if you can solve the problem.**
So let's dive deeper into how to find these ripe conditions for profit.

Distressed Properties

Many times, these properties jump out like a sore thumb — **if** you're paying attention.

When you're driving around, just keep your eyes open and be aware. You might see:

- Overgrown yards
- Boarded-up windows
- Piled-up mail or newspapers
- Broken fences
- Roofs that are obviously damaged
- Fire damage

- Or simply property that's clearly in need of serious maintenance

These are all signs that there are issues behind the scenes — and issues create opportunities.

The process is simple:

1. **Jot down the address.**
2. Go to the county courthouse or look up the county records online.
3. Find out who the owner is.
4. You'll see their name and the address where they receive the tax bill. (That's often different from the property address — which can tell you if it's an absentee owner.)

Since you're already at the courthouse (or online in county/city records), it's also not a bad idea to check for:

- **Code violations**
- **Nuisance properties**
- **Recorded complaints or liens**

Properties with code violations almost always have issues — sometimes big ones. And big issues can mean big discounts if you know what you're doing.

These are all direct, simple methods for finding good deals on distressed property.

Remember:
The property can't feed you if there's no food in the fridge.
If it's vacant, under-rented, mismanaged, or falling apart — that's your signal to step in and create value.

Distressed Owners

Just like homes have issues, **people** have issues.
And people's problems drive motivation.

It's almost always better to work with a **motivated seller** — someone who needs to sell, not just someone who casually wants to sell for top dollar.

Often, a person who only *wants* to sell will ask for too much money, and the deal won't be attractive for an investor. But a motivated seller has a problem that needs solving — and that's where you come in.

Distressed owners may be dealing with:

- Late payments
- Can't afford to keep the house up
- Tax delinquencies
- Foreclosure
- Bankruptcy
- Divorce
- Death in the family (probate situations)
- Health problems
- Job loss or reduced income
- Retirement
- Burnout from being a landlord

This is especially common with **out-of-state landlords** who are just tired of dealing with tenants and repairs from a distance.

When you're dealing with **multifamily property**, distressed owners may be facing:

- Weak rent rolls
- Many evictions
- Problem tenants
- High vacancy
- Bad or non-existent management

These deals aren't hard to find when you associate in the right circles and build real relationships.

You'll find clues to distressed owners by:

- Looking up public records (foreclosures, bankruptcies, tax liens, probates).
- Building relationships with **attorneys** (family law, probate, bankruptcy, eviction).
- Networking with other investors, agents, and property managers.

Whether it's the **property** or the **person** that's distressed, your job is simple:

Solve the problem.
Create the win.
Get the deal.

That's one of the main reasons my brokerage is called **Solid Real Estate Solutions** and why we use the slogan:

"We solve real estate problems."

Because when you know how to solve problems, you are *extremely valuable* —
and you **deserve to be compensated as such.**

Becoming a Deal Magnet

Off-market is where the **real** money is made.

Why?

- Everyone in the world isn't bidding on the same deal.
- The competition is lower.
- The spreads are bigger.
- Your creativity actually matters.

Most of these off-market deals come to you because of the **effort, energy, and image** you put out into the world.

Let the World Know Who You Are

First things first:

You must let **everybody** you come into contact with know that you:

- Solve real estate problems.
- Buy houses.
- Help people out of tight situations.
- Create win-win outcomes.

Even if they don't have a home to sell, it doesn't matter. People have friends, family, co-workers, church members, neighbors. They talk. And eventually, somebody in their world will have a real estate problem.

Bird Dogs & Finders' Fees

Tell people you'll pay a **finder's fee** if they bring you a deal that closes.
That's how you get bird dogs — people who keep their eyes and ears open and bring you opportunities.

Some people won't even care about the fee. They'll just be grateful you helped someone they know. Pay them anyway — or at least show appreciation with a gift, a dinner, or something meaningful.

Spending money is a sign of appreciation.
Paying people to help you is an awesome way to activate the **Law of Reciprocity.**

Brand Yourself as the Solution

While you're letting everyone know what you do, do it right:

- Carry business cards.
- Wrap or letter your vehicle so it acts as a moving billboard.
- Put bandit signs up (where legal) around town.
- Show up at networking events and investor meetups.
- Be present, visible, and consistent.

You want to become that person everyone thinks of when they hear the words:

"We need to sell this place, but we've got a problem…"

Invest in Attracting Deals

If you really want your business to thrive, invest in marketing:

- Use **direct mail** to targeted lists (absentee owners, pre-foreclosures, tax delinquents, etc.).
- Hire a **VA** to do cold calling.
- Post regularly on **social media** about what you do, the problems you solve, and success stories (while respecting privacy and compliance).

The more energy you put into letting the world know who you are and how you help, the more that **river of wealth** flows in your direction.

That's just the **Law of Universal Influence** in action.

Deals, like water, **flow toward the exit where they're directed.** Your energy, focus, and presence are the channels that direct them.

Hunting Opportunities with Purpose

While off-market is the goldmine, we don't want to sleep on those who are publicly waving a flag that says:

"Hey, I'm selling. Please help."

Even though it's not as common to find **home run** deals in the advertised space, they're still out there — especially when you know what to look for.

Because of the realm of possibility we live in, you may be able to see value and opportunity where others don't.

Remember: you're being trained to think like a **real estate expert** now.

So step into that identity… and act like it.

Watch the MLS

The MLS is still a powerful tool when used correctly.

Watch for:

- **Expired listings**
- **Aged properties** (on the market 60+ days)
- Multiple **price reductions**
- Language like "**motivated seller**, "**needs TLC**," or "**as-is**"

It's very common for someone with an expired listing to accept a lower offer than they turned down in the past — especially if time, stress, and carrying costs have worn them down.

You can't be afraid to ask for what you want, because how can you get anything if you don't ask?

That's not just a principle —
that's biblical:

"Ask and you shall receive."

Most importantly, **write fast offers.**

Money loves speed.
And hesitation blocks the flow of wealth because **money rewards action.**

If you're not at least a little embarrassed by your first offer, it's probably too high.

Look Beyond the MLS

In addition to the MLS, search wherever sellers might advertise:

- Craigslist
- LoopNet
- Crexi
- BiggerPockets Marketplace
- Facebook Marketplace
- Local investor groups
- For Sale By Owner (FSBO) signs stuck in yards or taped to windows
- Community bulletin boards

A lot of motivated sellers don't want to pay agents or don't know where else to go, so they post in places like Craigslist or eBay, or just stick a sign in their yard.

Some of the best opportunities are hiding in plain sight.

Build Relationships with People in the Game

Relationships are everything in this business.

Build connections with:

- **Real estate agents** who understand investment deals. Tell them exactly what you're looking for.
- **Mortgage brokers** who may hear about deals before they hit the market.

- **Contractors, handymen, and tradespeople** who are often the first to know when a property is falling apart or an owner is running out of money.
- **Other investors** — not as competition, but as future business partners.

Pocket listings come from agents who **know and trust you.** Deals get shared back and forth between investors all the time. Joint ventures are born in conversations over coffee, not contracts alone.

Those other investors are not your enemies.
They are your future collaborators.

The most important thing here is your **integrity**.

- Do what you say you're going to do.
- Don't pretend you can do what you can't.
- Don't burn bridges over greed or ego.

Your integrity is extremely valuable.

If you lose it, you're destined to fail — because this business runs on **trust.**

Creative Control Through OPM (Other People's Money)

Now that you know how to **find** deals, it's time to talk about how to **control** them.

Remember this:

Ownership is optional. Control is everything.

Yes, you can always use traditional methods:

- Submit your down payment to the title company or attorney.
- Get a conventional, FHA, VA, or commercial loan.
- Use a 1031 exchange to roll equity into the next property.

Those are valid strategies — but that's not what this chapter is about.

This chapter is about opening the doors of **creativity** and solving problems in ways that most people never think of.

Here are some of the tools of **creative investors** — the people who prefer using **OPM (Other People's Money)** instead of their own.

Land Contracts, Options & Lease Options

These structures are in the **rent-to-own family.**

You might:

- Rent or lease the property from the owner.
- Negotiate an option to purchase it later at a set or formula-based price.
- **Record** that option at the courthouse to secure your equitable interest.

That recording is extremely important because it:

- Protects your position.
- Prevents the seller from selling the property out from under you.
- Gives you leverage and control over the eventual sale.

Done properly, this allows you to control valuable assets with a fraction of the cost of traditional financing.

Assignments & Wholesaling

Assignments and wholesaling are where a lot of investors get their start. I certainly did.

The steps are simple:

1. Get the property under contract at a good price.
2. Make sure the contract is **assignable.**
3. Be transparent with the seller and let them know you may close with one of your business partners.
4. Take that good deal to another investor — and sell them your **contract**, not the property.
5. Collect an assignment fee at closing.

You never actually own the property — you own the **right** to buy it, and you sell that right for a profit.

On my first investment deal, I found **two triplexes** and put them under contract for **$150,000 each**. I brought them to an investor who thought it was a great deal at **$175,000 each**.

I sold them the contracts, pocketed **$50,000**, and did it all within a month.
They even advanced me some money before the deal closed.

I was so excited. I had the real estate bug. I knew this was what I was meant to do.

There's something special about the first deal.

It's like when your eyes open in the morning — it's a brand-new day and you're ready to hit the road running.

One important rule in wholesaling and assignments:

Don't be greedy. Leave profit for the buyer.

They're your partners in this game, not your victims.
We're building long-term relationships here — this is not a "hit it and quit it" thing.

When you leave some meat on the bone for your buyer:

- You create a strong, loyal relationship.
- You become valuable to every investor they talk to.
- Word of mouth travels.

It's like ripples in a pond.
That's the ripple effect.

Seller Financing

Seller financing is another powerful tool.

Here, the seller becomes the bank.

You:

- Agree on the purchase price.
- Negotiate the down payment.
- Set the interest rate and terms.
- Often include a **balloon payment** after a set number of years.

This works great with:

- Free and clear properties.
- Older sellers who want income without headaches.
- Sellers facing tax consequences who don't want all the money at once.

Ask the seller what they actually **need** — and structure a solution that meets both of your goals.

Subject-To (Taking Over Existing Loans)

I absolutely love this strategy.

With a **subject-to** deal, you:

- Take title to the property.
- Keep the existing loan in place.
- Bring the payments current if needed.
- Start making payments in place of the seller.

The loan remains in the seller's name, but you control the property.

The risk here is the **due-on-sale clause**, which appears in most mortgages and gives the bank the right (not the obligation) to call the loan due if the title transfers.

Many investors handle this by:

- Getting **title insurance** to make sure the title is clean.
- Structuring the transfer through a **trust** with the help of a competent attorney.

Under the **Garn–St. Germain Act of 1982**, certain transfers into trust are protected from triggering the due-on-sale clause when structured correctly.

One approach is:

1. The owner moves the property into a trust.
2. A deed is recorded at the courthouse showing the property is now owned by that trust.
3. You then purchase the **beneficial interest** of the trust — not the property directly.
4. The deed remains in the name of the trust, not yours personally.

When I bought property this way, I named the trust after the property address, for clarity:

"The 123 Main St Trust"

This may sound complicated, but there are attorneys who do this regularly. The key is to respect the law, respect the structure, and respect the power of this strategy.

Loans (Non-Traditional) — Private Money, Hard Money & Creative Capital

There are plenty of ways to get money outside of traditional bank loans.

Some are more expensive. Some are not.
The key is to understand the **cost of money** and how it fits into the overall deal.

- **Private money** is borrowing from individuals — often hands-off investors who want a return but don't want to swing a hammer or manage tenants.
- **Hard money** is typically based on the **value of the property after it's repaired** (ARV). It's usually more expensive, but fast and easier to qualify for because it's asset-driven, not credit-score-driven.

I once bought a property using a **credit card check** and didn't have to pay interest on that money for 18 months. That gave me plenty of time to add value and refinance the loan if I wanted to.

Creativity + knowledge + integrity = power.

Equity Sharing & Partnerships

Equity sharing and partnerships are another way to buy property without using your own money.

If your credit is bad, partner with someone who has **good credit.**
If your bank account is low, partner with someone who has **capital.**

You:

- Find the deal.
- Do the work.
- Manage the process.

They:

- Help you fund it.
- Bring their credit, cash, or experience to the table.

You split the profits.
That's a **win-win deal**.

But there's a catch:

You will not attract good partners if you are not a person of integrity.

I've said this before, and I'll say it again because it matters that much:

Your integrity is the most valuable asset you have when working with others.

As you can see, there is so much possible through creativity and using other people's money.

You don't need capital.
You don't need perfect credit.

You need:

- Creativity
- Knowledge
- Integrity
- And a reputation for solving problems.

Creativity with Enhanced Vision

This section is for the more advanced investors — those with **enhanced vision.**

This is about acquiring property by **creating** what doesn't even exist yet.

One way of acquiring the right property is to **build it**.

Look for:

- **Infill opportunities** — open lots or unused pieces of land between existing homes inside the city.
- Land that can be **rezoned** or **re-entitled** for higher and better use.
- Sites where you can add:
    - A garage conversion
    - An ADU in the backyard
    - A duplex out of what used to be a single-family house
    - Condos out of an old hotel
    - Apartments out of an old school or commercial building

You can increase the **value of land** by:

- Building on it.
- Placing a mobile home, manufactured home, or modular building (where allowed).
- Re-imagining what it can be.

Anything is possible with vision.

I'm one of the owners of **3D Real Estate Developers**, and we own a 3D printer capable of pouring concrete and building a structure within a few days.

That's what I mean by enhanced vision.

Keep an open mind.
Because with vision, if you can conceive it — you can achieve it.

Summary

Now you know:

- Where all the good deals are.
- How to attract them.
- How to hunt them down with purpose.
- How to control them using OPM.
- How to get creative with advanced strategies.
- How to see opportunity where others only see problems.

You also know that bigger projects often require a **team**.

For now, just pay attention to what's going on in your mind.

You should have ideas bouncing all over the place like a pinball ricocheting off the bumpers in the machine. You may be thinking about:

- What actions you can take.
- How you want to present yourself.
- What kind of investor you are becoming.

Most importantly, it needs to be about your **identity.**

Say this to yourself:

I am a real estate investor.
I solve other people's problems.
I attract opportunity.
I am full of creativity.
I am a magnet for wealth.
I attract the right people and build a strong real estate investment team.

This chapter is just the start.

In the next chapter, we're going to discuss **building that team** and taking this business to the next level.

Next up:

Chapter 10 — Raising Capital Through Connection and Integrity.

CHAPTER 10

RAISING CAPITAL THROUGH CONNECTION AND INTEGRITY

Which came first — the chicken or the egg?
The deal or the money?

Who cares?
It doesn't matter anyway…
as long as we get to eat the breakfast.

Because in real estate, both the chicken and the egg show up when you're the kind of investor people want to do business with.

Money doesn't chase opportunity.
The river of wealth flows toward the person whose energy influences the current.

People don't invest in spreadsheets — they invest in people.
Yes, they need the spreadsheets.
They absolutely expect you to know how to read them.
Spreadsheets alone won't get you funded.

To attract real money, you must become the kind of leader who has:

- The knowledge
- The mindset
- The ability to take action with certainty

This chapter is where you learn how to become that leader.

This is where you learn the truth:
Raising capital isn't about raising money…
it's about building relationships.

Let's begin.

The Secret Truths About Raising Capital

If you're reading this because you're ready to play bigger — good.
Because bigger deals require one thing:

Other people's money.

First Truth:

"If you have a fear of spending money, you will telegraph that fear… and others will fear spending money with you."

Money responds to emotion.
Money responds to courage.
Money responds to clarity.
Money responds to leadership.

When you carry fear or hesitation around money, people feel it instantly — even if they can't explain why.

Fear blocks the flow of money.
Confidence directs it.

Second Truth:

"Money does not chase opportunity — it flows toward the energy that attracts it."

Investors aren't looking for spreadsheets.
They **NEED** spreadsheets.
But spreadsheets alone aren't enough.

A spreadsheet can't lead anyone.
A spreadsheet can't calm fear.
A spreadsheet can't inspire confidence.
A spreadsheet can't build trust.
A spreadsheet can't create alignment.

People invest in **YOU**.

They want a leader who:

- Understands the math
- Understands the market
- Understands the mindset
- Understands integrity
- Understands responsibility
- And understands how to communicate clearly and confidently

In this world, you're not selling deals — you're selling belief.

Investors want to believe:

- You know the road
- You know how to navigate obstacles
- And most of all: you'll do exactly what you say you'll do

When investors trust you and see that you know the road to success, they want to travel with you on that road.

This chapter is about:

- Identity
- Communication
- Presence
- Integrity
- Competence
- And leadership

Because raising capital is an identity-based skill.

People don't follow spreadsheets.
People follow energy.
People follow certainty.
People follow vision.

And money follows them.

Understanding Investor Types

Money comes from people.
People come with expectations.
Expectations come with rules.
And rules come with consequences.

So you MUST know the difference between investor types — especially if you're new.

This section is intentionally heavy, deep, and clear.
Think of it as your real-world capital foundation.

1. Passive Investors

A) Accredited Investors

Accredited investors are individuals legally recognized as financially sophisticated.

They qualify in one of these ways:

- $200k+ annual income individually (last 2 years)
- $300k+ annual income jointly (last 2 years)
- $1M net worth (excluding primary residence)
- Certain financial licenses (Series 7, 65, 82)

Why accredited investors matter:

- You can market to them publicly (506(c))
- They can invest in deals others cannot
- They move faster
- They require less hand-holding

- They tend to reinvest

Accredited investors LOVE clarity and confidence.
They fund YOU — not the spreadsheet.

They are the highway lanes of real estate capital.

B) Sophisticated Investors

Sophisticated investors understand risk and financial documents but may not meet accredited net-worth thresholds.

They usually:

- Have investing experience
- Understand real estate or stocks
- Can read a Private Placement Memorandum (PPM)
- Know financial terminology
- Are comfortable with risk

Why they matter:

Under **506(b)**, you can accept sophisticated investors **only** if you have a pre-existing substantive relationship.

Meaning:

- You know them
- They know you
- You understand their financial profile
- You've spoken about investments before

Key Rule:
You CANNOT publicly advertise deals to sophisticated investors.

Think of them as "almost accredited" — and one good property cycle can turn them into accredited investors.

C) Neither Accredited nor Sophisticated

These individuals:

- Don't understand investment risk
- Don't understand financial statements
- Don't meet regulatory qualifications

If someone is neither:
They cannot invest passively in securities-based real estate offerings.

They *can* participate in:

- Joint ventures (if they are active)
- Equity splits where they materially contribute
- Certain creative deal structures

But they cannot legally be passive investors in a syndication.

This is vital — get this wrong, and you violate securities laws.

2. Joint Venture (JV) Partners

JV partners are **active participants**, not passive.

A true JV partner:

- Makes decisions

- Shares responsibility
- Has voting power
- Is part of operations

If someone gives money but is passive…

That is NOT a JV.

That is a **security**.

Call it a JV when it isn't — and you're inviting lawsuits.

3. Limited Partners (LPs)

LPs are passive investors in syndications.

They:

- Invest capital
- Receive distributions
- Own equity
- Have limited liability
- Have no involvement in operations

LPs want:

- Clear communication
- Predictability
- Transparency
- Professionalism

Many LP offerings qualify for Regulation D exemptions. But even when exempt, sponsors must meet SEC disclosure obligations.

LP money is the backbone of larger commercial deals.

Why This Section Matters

New investors get in trouble because they:

- Treat all investors the same
- Mislabel passive investors as JVs
- Use the wrong documentation
- Don't follow SEC rules
- Pitch strangers illegally

This section protects your deals, your future, your partners, and your reputation.

Now let's go deeper.

Compliance: Doing It Right

Compliance isn't optional.
Compliance is protection.

Compliance protects:

- You
- Your business
- Your partners
- Your future
- And every investor who trusts you

1. Syndication = Securities Offering

If someone invests passively:

- You are selling a security
- SEC rules apply
- Federal consequences exist

This is non-negotiable.

2. The Two Most Common Offerings

A. 506(b)

- No public advertising
- Unlimited accredited investors
- Up to 35 sophisticated investors
- Pre-existing relationship required

B. 506(c)

- Public advertising allowed
- Accredited investors only
- Third-party verification required

Know which offering your deal falls under.
Ignorance is not a defense.

3. The PPM (Private Placement Memorandum)

"The PPM is the document that protects YOU and protects THEM."

It outlines:

- Risks
- Fees
- Structure
- Distributions
- Strategy
- Legal disclosures

If anything ever goes wrong, the PPM proves transparency and integrity.

4. The Cardinal Rule

Never promise a return. Ever.
Not even if the deal looks bulletproof.

You may present:

- Projections
- Scenarios
- Historical data

But you never guarantee.

5. Bring the Attorney In Early

Professionals respect professionalism.
Bringing your attorney in early is leadership — not weakness.

It tells investors:

"You're safe with me."

Creating Irresistible Offerings: Deal Structuring

You're not just raising money.
You're creating a **wealth vehicle**.

The structure must align with:

- Investor goals
- Project timelines
- Risk
- Market conditions
- Your track record
- Exit strategy

Here are the key components:

1. The Pro Forma

Your pro forma is your **numerical story**, not just a spreadsheet.

A strong pro forma includes:

- Actual rent roll
- Actual operating expenses
- Market rents
- Renovation budget
- Timeline to stabilization
- Cash-on-cash return

- IRR
- Equity multiple
- CapEx plan
- Market comps

A weak pro forma kills deals instantly.

2. The Pitch Deck

Your pitch deck is your **visual credibility.**

Include:

- Photos
- Value-add opportunities
- Market data
- Team biographies
- Financial projections
- Exit strategies
- Risk mitigation

Remember:
Information is 50%.
Energy is the other 50%.

3. The Operating Agreement

This is the rulebook.

It defines:

- Roles
- Responsibilities
- Voting rights
- Distributions
- Decision-making
- Conflict resolution

Serious investors scrutinize this document closely.

4. The Investor Funnel

A professional funnel includes:

- Intake form
- Call #1: Connection + Assessment
- Call #2: Deal Presentation
- Email follow-up
- Commitment form
- Wiring instructions (sent securely)
- Closing coordination

A clear process builds trust.

Why Investors Actually Say Yes

Decisions are not made logically.
They are made emotionally.

Money is not the goal —
money is the vehicle of appreciation for the opportunity.

Investors do NOT say yes because:

- You have a spreadsheet
- You have a pitch deck
- You memorized a perfect script

They say yes because:

- You're confident
- You're competent
- You're transparent
- You communicate clearly
- You move with integrity
- You see the path
- You calm their fears
- You radiate the right energy

And…

We don't chase money — we attract partners.
If everyone doesn't win, it's not a good deal.
If your name carries weight, raising money becomes effortless.

And finally:

After someone completes a sweet deal with you…
they come back for more with the same enthusiasm a baby has when he wants that second spoon of ice cream.

Because success feels good — and people return to what feels good.

Summary

Now you know:

- How investors think
- How compliance works
- How offerings must be structured
- How confidence attracts money
- How to build relationships that last
- How to speak the language investors trust

You're not chasing money.
You're becoming the person money flows toward — naturally.

And now…

You're ready for the next level.

When you master raising capital, the next question becomes:

How do you choose the right partners?
Not just anyone with money…
but those who align with your values, your energy, and your long-term vision.

That's what's next.

Chapter 11: Partnerships & Teams — Vision, Value & Harmony
Let's go build the team that turns opportunities into empires.

CHAPTER 11

PARTNERSHIPS & TEAMS: VISION, VALUE & HARMONY

A ship with an aligned crew sails smooth and steady.
A ship with one misaligned sailor can drift off course, crash into the rocks, overturn in chaos, or sink beneath the weight of confusion.

Real estate works the same way.

Behind every profitable project is alignment.
Behind every disaster is misalignment.

Partnerships are leverage.
Teams are leverage.
Alignment is everything.

And nothing taught me this more clearly than the mistake I'm about to share with you.

The Energy of Alignment

The Cost of Misalignment

Here is a great example of how I chose the wrong team member and paid for it.
My errors are your lessons… choose your team wisely.

Years ago, I found a 3-bedroom property in Western Maryland — a perfect long-term buy-and-hold play.

I didn't want to tie up my cash, so I acquired this property creatively:
I bought it using a 0% interest credit-card check, giving me exactly **18 months** to stabilize the asset and refinance before the rate changed.

That meant:

✓ repairs needed to happen fast

✓ cash flow needed to stabilize fast

✓ and the timeline had to stay tight

On paper, everything worked.

Until I picked the wrong person for the job.

The agent who sold me the property said she was also a property manager.
Seemed convenient.
Seemed trustworthy.
So I let her manage it.

When she told me the property needed repairs, I said, "Great — let's get it fixed."
She said she had a "great handyman."

Months went by… repair after repair… bill after bill… and the property felt like a money pit.
Every time I thought we'd caught up, something else "came up."

Eventually, I flew from California to Maryland to see what was going on.

And that's when I discovered the truth:

The agent who sold me the property, who claimed to be managing it, was also **dating the handyman she kept hiring**.

She made money on:

✓ the sale

✓ the management fees

✓ and the inflated repair costs she funneled to her boyfriend

Conflicts of interest everywhere.
Misalignment everywhere.
And my 18-month clock was ticking.

This wasn't a "bad team member."

This was three jobs filled by one misaligned person:

- agent
- manager
- contractor

One weak link → three broken systems.
One weak link → my entire strategy compromised.

The lesson?

One misaligned partner, contractor, or team member can sabotage your plan, your profit, and your peace of mind.

Alignment isn't optional.

Alignment is survival.

What Alignment Actually Means

Alignment isn't about everyone being the same.
Alignment is about everyone rowing in the same direction — toward the same destination — with no hidden agendas.

In real estate, alignment has three components:

1. Shared Values

Integrity
Honesty
Transparency
Responsibility
Follow-through

If they don't share these, the partnership is already doomed.

2. Shared Vision

Everyone must see the same mission:

- Are we flipping?
- Are we holding long-term?
- Are we maximizing cash flow or equity?
- Are we taking fast action or slow precision?

Different visions create chaos.

3. Shared Intent

Intent is the silent force behind every action.

My intent with that Maryland property was long-term stability.
Her intent was short-term extraction.

Intent matters more than words.
Intent shapes energy.
Intent reveals alignment.

When intent diverges, results collapse.

Partners and How to Vet Them

Your partners amplify your strengths **or** multiply your weaknesses.

There are only two types of partners:

A. The Right Partner

They solve problems
They honor agreements
They tell the truth, even when it's hard
They bring skills you don't have
They make you stronger
They focus on win-win outcomes

B. The Wrong Partner

They drain your energy
They create confusion

They hide information
They delay decisions
They bring drama instead of value
They focus on themselves, not the deal

How to Vet a Partner

A partner must be tested on four levels:

1. Character

Do they keep their word?
Do they own their mistakes?
Do they do what they say?
Do their actions align with their image?
Would you trust them with your money — and your family's money?

2. Competence

Do they know what they're doing?
Do they have experience?
Do they follow systems?
Do they communicate clearly?
Do they add value equal to their equity?
Competence prevents chaos.
Incompetence creates it.

3. Chemistry

Do you work well together?

Do you communicate easily?
Can you disagree without disrespect?
Are they emotionally stable?

Chemistry is the oil in the engine.

4. Contribution

What do they bring to the table?

Skill?
Money?
Network?
Knowledge?
Labor?
Leadership?

Every partner must bring value that multiplies the mission.

The Crew: Building Your Team

Partnerships are one thing.
Teams are another.

Your team includes:

- Property managers
- Agents
- Contractors
- Handymen
- Lenders
- Inspectors

- Attorneys
- Transaction coordinators
- Bookkeepers
- Virtual assistants
- Bird dogs

One misaligned teammate can cost you:

- money
- time
- reputation
- stability
- your entire project

A ship with an aligned crew sails smooth.
A ship with one misaligned sailor can drift off course, crash into the rocks, overturn in chaos, or sink beneath the weight of confusion.

It's not poetic — it's real.

How to Vet a Team Member

Look for:

✓ Transparency

✓ Prompt communication

✓ Documentation

✓ Clarity in estimates

✓ Proof of work

✓ Real references

✓ No excuses

✓ No hidden relationships

✓ No emotional volatility

Red flags appear early.
Trust them.

Leadership: Harmony in Action

Leadership is not doing everything yourself.
Leadership is being the captain who:

- sets the direction
- communicates the mission
- scans the horizon
- reads the waters
- sees storms before the crew does
- and aligns the team toward the destination

Your job is not to hold every rope.
Your job is to guide the crew with vision and wisdom.

Your crew needs:

- A clear mission
- A clear destination
- A clear timeline
- A clear standard

And they take their cues from you.

Leadership is alignment in motion.

Alignment creates harmony.
Harmony breeds wealth.

Partnerships grow your empire.
Teams protect your empire.
Alignment multiplies your empire.

Because when alignment is present:

Communication is sharp
Execution is fast
Problems dissolve quickly
Stress stays low
Profit stays high
And energy flows in one direction

When alignment is absent:

Timelines collapse
Costs explode
Arguments ignite
Motives clash
And the entire project slides sideways

Alignment is a powerful magnifier of wealth.

And misalignment is the hidden destroyer of it.

Summary

Now you understand:

Why alignment determines outcomes

- The wrong teammate can derail everything
- The wrong partner can sabotage profit
- Intent matters more than talent

What alignment requires

- Shared values
- Shared vision
- Shared intent
- Complementary strengths

How to vet partners and team members

- Character
- Competence
- Chemistry
- Contribution

Why leadership sets the tone

- The captain determines the course
- The crew follows the energy
- Vision drives velocity

Why alignment multiplies wealth

When everyone rows together, the ship moves faster, smoother, and farther.

And when one sailor rows against the current…
the whole ship feels it.

Your math is solid.

Your negotiation skills are aligned.
Your partnerships and team foundation are strong.

Now it's time to master the mental models that separate average investors from extraordinary ones.

Let's build the mind of a deal-maker.

Time to move to PART IV — The Wealth System - Building More than a Portfolio
Chapter 12 — The FFL Deal-Maker Academy (Mental Models That Win)

PART IV

THE WEALTH SYSTEM

BUILDING MORE THAN A PORTFOLIO

CHAPTER 12

THE FFL DEAL-MAKER ACADEMY (MENTAL MODELS THAT WIN)

Most people chase deals.
Deal-makers create them.

Let me show you exactly what I mean.

I once visited family on the East Coast, in a quiet little town most people had written off as "too depressed" to invest in. Small rundown houses. Struggling businesses. Locals convinced nothing good could happen there.

To most people:
a dead market.
To me:
opportunity everywhere.

Why?

Because when I looked around, I didn't just see poor neighborhoods and beaten houses…
I saw equations.

Low prices + (low income) rental demand = cash-flow potential.

While everyone else was saying:

"There's no money in this town,"

I was saying:

"This place is undervalued — and misunderstood."

So I put up bandit signs all over the city.

And guess what happened?

I started getting call after call…
lead after lead…
and within a short period of time…

I owned six properties in that "dead" town.

This is the difference between the average investor and the strategic investor.

They saw a problem.
I saw a pattern.

They saw a depressed market.
I saw a marketplace full of renters and tons of potential.

They saw low income.
I saw low competition.

They saw risk.
I saw profit.

That's what this chapter is about:

The mental models that turn ordinary investors into deal-makers — the kind who create opportunity where it appears none exists.

Let's begin.

The Deal-Maker Identity

(Seeing What Others Miss)

Before we talk math, formulas, or frameworks, we must talk identity — because the difference between a deal-chaser and a deal-maker is how they think.

Deal-chasers look for "good markets."
Deal-makers look for good mechanics.

Deal-chasers need perfect conditions.
Deal-makers create profitable conditions.

Deal-chasers wait.
Deal-makers move.

A deal-maker lives by one core belief:

Value is always present — if you know how to see it.

So let's sharpen the lenses that allow you to see it.

The "Problem → Pattern → Perspective → Profit" Model

Every deal-maker uses this mental model — consciously or unconsciously:

1. PROBLEM
What's wrong?
What does everyone complain about?
What do others assume is impossible?

2. PATTERN
Where is this happening repeatedly?
Is the "problem" actually a predictable condition?

3. PERSPECTIVE
How can you see this differently than the crowd?
What's the angle no one else is taking or everyone else is missing?

4. PROFIT
What value emerges from the new perspective?
Where is the money in the misalignment?

In my East Coast story:
Problem → depressed town
Pattern → high renter demand + low supply
Perspective → not "bad market," but "undervalued entry point"
Profit → buy, rehab, refi & hold

This model works in every market cycle, every asset class, and every stage of your career.

When you master these four steps, you stop relying on luck…

and start creating opportunity.

Strategic Mental Models

(The Tools Deal-Makers Think With)

These are the mental frameworks wealth builders use automatically — the architecture of strategic thinking.

1. The Leverage Model

Deal-makers ask one question:

"What creates the highest return on my time, energy, and relationships?"

Their answers typically break down like this:

Learn the language → high return
Build relationships → high return
Analyze deals → high return

Visit every property personally → low return
Swing a hammer yourself → almost zero return
Do everything alone → negative return

Leverage is choosing the activities that compound wealth — and delegating the rest.

2. The Value Stack Model

A deal-maker doesn't ask:
"How do I win this deal?"

They ask:
"How do I stack value so everyone wins?"

Value stacking creates deals where:

- sellers get relief
- partners get profit
- investors get clarity
- contractors get consistency
- property managers get alignment
- YOU get long-term wealth

When you create more value for more people…
opportunity chases YOU.

3. The Five-Steps-to-Yes Model

Deal-makers understand momentum-driven decision-making.

1. **Clarity** (what the deal IS)
2. **Alignment** (what everyone needs)
3. **Safety** (remove fears & unknowns)
4. **Opportunity** (show the upside clearly)
5. **Simplicity** (make the path easy)

When you hit all five…
"Let me think about it" becomes "When do we start?"

4. The Exit-First Strategy

Deal-makers NEVER start with the purchase.

They start with:

- the exit
- the timeline
- the risk
- the capital plan
- the end vision

If you can't see the exit…
you don't have a deal.

This single mental model has saved investors millions.

The FFL Wealth Operating Lens

(The Deal-Maker's Inner Compass)

Your FFL modality becomes a decision-making weapon here:

FAITH — Vision and Forward Projection

Deal-makers ask:
"What can this become?"

They see potential.
They forecast accurately.
They believe in their ability to execute.

Faith is not hope.
Faith is a disciplined projection.

FORGIVENESS — Data Reset + Removing Bias

Deal-makers don't cling to:

- sunk costs
- past mistakes
- emotional attachment

They reset fast.
They adapt without ego.
They make decisions from clarity — not wounds.

LOVE — Presence + Emotional Intelligence

This isn't soft.
This is power.

Love means:

- caring about the relationship
- caring about the team
- caring about the outcome for everyone

Deal-makers who operate from Love become magnets for collaboration.

This FFL lens upgrades every decision you make.

The Investor Compass

(Your True-North Framework)

Every real estate empire stays aligned by following the four directional pillars:

NORTH — Long-Term Wealth

You're not doing transactions…
You're building a legacy.

SOUTH — Cash Flow Stability

Does this deal pay you?
Does it sustain your business?

EAST — Credibility + Relationships

Who you are matters more than what you buy.

WEST — Systems + Repeatability

If it can't be repeated…
It can't scale.

Summary

Now you know the mental models that make you a deal-maker:

- The Problem → Pattern → Perspective → Profit Method
- The Leverage Model
- The Value Stack
- The Five-Steps-to-Yes Model
- The Exit-First Strategy
- The FFL Lens
- The Investor Compass

This is the inner architecture of real estate mastery.

With these tools, you no longer hope for opportunities…
You create them.

Next up:
Chapter 13 — The Road to Abundant Wealth
Where we turn these mental models into systems…
And systems into wealth.

CHAPTER 13

THE ROAD TO ABUNDANT WEALTH

BUILDING THE SYSTEMS THAT MAKE SUCCESS INEVITABLE

Most investors fumble their way through real estate like I once fumbled through the touchscreen of my Tesla.

I remember the moment clearly.

I was driving at night, the high beams kept blasting on and off, and I could not for the life of me figure out how to adjust them. I kept poking around the touchscreen… sliding through menus… tapping the wrong icons… opening windows I did not need… and wasting precious focus on something that should have been simple.

All I needed to do was search the owner's manual.

But I did not.

I spent ten minutes guessing, fumbling, getting frustrated, and making the drive harder than it needed to be — simply because I did not know the system.

Most investors operate the same way.

They poke buttons.
Guess.
Try random strategies.

Take course after course after course.
Hope they do not crash the car.

When what they really need is **a system that shows them exactly what to do… exactly when to do it… and exactly why it works.**

And that is what this chapter is about.

Most real estate books give you:

- a cheat sheet
- a floor plan
- or a highlight reel of tactics

But this chapter gives you the **entire blueprint package**:

- The plans
- The elevations
- The structural engineering
- The compliance steps
- The electrical layout
- The plumbing pathways
- The sequencing
- The workflow
- The functions
- The systems

Everything you need to take a project — or a business — all the way to the finish line.

Because this is not just the owner's manual…

This is the roadmap.
The machine.

The operational engine behind real estate wealth.

Let's build it.

Building Systems That Scale (*Your Wealth Machine*)

Most investors never scale because they operate like one-person construction crews — doing every task themselves, trying to run every tool, and burning out long before the foundation is cured.

Deal-makers operate differently.

They build **systems**, not stress.

A system is:

- a repeatable sequence
- a predictable outcome
- a set of instructions
- a standard of execution
- a process someone else can run
- a machine that works the same every time

Here are the core systems you MUST build if you want a business that grows without consuming your life.

1. The Lead Acquisition System

This is the lifeblood of your entire operation.

Your system must generate:

- seller leads
- agent connections

- investor conversations
- partner opportunities
- off-market deals

And it must do it **consistently**, not randomly.

The system should include:

- inbound methods
- outbound methods
- follow-up automation
- relationship cycles
- weekly review metrics

When this system is healthy, you never worry about "finding deals" because your pipeline never stops flowing.

2. The Deal Analysis System

This system eliminates emotional decision-making.

It ensures:

- you run the numbers the same way every time
- you objectively evaluate risk
- you calculate exits before offers
- you understand the 5–10 variables that determine success

Your analysis pipeline should include:

- initial quick scan
- financial breakdown
- risk grid
- exit-first evaluation

- decision threshold (buy / maybe / no)

This system will save you from more bad deals than anything else in your toolbox.

3. The Offer & Negotiation System

Most investors wing this part.

Deal-makers do not.

A negotiation system includes:

- pre-framing the conversation
- identifying challenges, not objections
- alignment language
- pacing → leading sequences
- the discovery loop
- the "yes-if" reframing
- clear decision pathways
- emotional safety checks

When your negotiation system is dialed in, deals become smoother, faster, and more profitable — with far less resistance.

4. The Due Diligence System

This is where amateurs get burned and professionals get rich.

Your system must include:

- physical inspections
- tenant-behavior scans
- vendor verification

- compliance flags
- document and title checks
- timeline protections
- repair estimates
- risk reserves

Due diligence is not paperwork.
It is **protection**.

A strong DD system protects your future cash flow and your reputation.

5. The Renovation & Value-Add System

This is where money is made or lost.

A systemized renovation plan includes:

- scope clarity
- budget confirmations
- contractor schedules
- payment structures
- quality checks
- weekly reporting
- contingency buffers
- accountability rules

When done right, renovations multiply wealth.
When done wrong, they destroy it.

6. The Management System

Great management creates generational wealth.

Poor management destroys it.

Your system should include:

- tenant placement standards
- communication expectations
- reporting formats
- emergency protocols
- repair routing
- contractor hierarchy
- renewal guidelines
- eviction thresholds

Management is not glamorous.

But it is one of the biggest wealth multipliers in the business.

7. The Review & Feedback Loop

This is the difference between running a project…

…and running a business.

Every month you evaluate:

- what worked
- what failed
- where money leaked
- where time was wasted
- what needs to be automated
- which team members elevated the system

- which ones weakened it

This loop upgrades your system every cycle — making the entire machine more efficient.

When these seven systems come together, your business becomes **scalable, predictable, and unstoppable**.

This is the foundation of your operational roadmap.

Let's keep building.

Strategic Alliances & Long-Term Relationships (*Your Expansion Engine*)

Real estate is not a solo sport.

Your "team" is not optional.
Your "alliances" are not extras.

Your alliances ARE the velocity of your business.

Let's break it down.

1. The Agent Alliance System

Agents are your intel.

They see deals before anyone else.
They hear whispers long before they hit the market.
They know the sellers, the timelines, the pressures, the fears, the motivations.

Your system must:

- build relationships with the right agents
- reward them with repeat business
- give them clarity on your criteria
- keep communication crisp
- stay high-trust and low-maintenance

When an agent knows you are serious, decisive, and fair…
you become their first call.

2. The Lender Alliance System

Lenders determine speed and scale.

You need:

- traditional lenders
- relationship lenders
- private lenders
- creative finance allies

And each must know:

- your strategy
- your timelines
- your financial patterns
- your communication style
- your track record

When lenders trust you, money becomes easy — and fast.

3. The Contractor & Renovation Alliance System

This is where investors rise or fall.

Your system must:

- vet contractors thoroughly
- confirm expertise, not claims
- structure payment milestones
- insist on weekly reports
- standardize scopes
- protect against corner-cutting
- track performance

A great contractor multiplies your wealth.
A bad one erases it.

4. The Property Management Alliance System

Property managers are the "operators of your vision."

They:

- protect your cash flow
- maintain your asset
- handle your tenants
- enforce your standards
- stabilize your business

Your system must:

- define expectations clearly
- monitor performance
- track response times

- ensure alignment
- evaluate quarterly

When your PM is aligned, doors stay full, problems stay small, and wealth accelerates.

5. The Investor & Partner Alliance System

Partners are accelerants.

Right partner → growth and synergy
Wrong partner → chaos and collapse

Your system must include:

- vetting values
- vetting vision
- vetting timelines
- vetting integrity
- vetting alignment
- vetting communication style
- vetting emotional maturity

One misaligned partner can topple the entire structure — like a single weak beam in a building.

Your alliances ARE your architecture.

Build wisely.

Automation & Efficiency in Real Estate (*Doing More with Less Energy*)

You do not scale by doing more work.

You scale by building better **systems** that do the work for you.

Automation is not technology.

Automation is:

- clarity
- repeatability
- delegation
- flow
- relief
- acceleration

Here are the major automation systems your business must build:

1. Lead Flow Automation

Your lead machine should run:

- daily
- predictably
- without your constant energy

Automate:

- follow-ups
- reminders
- message sequences
- status tracking

- pipeline management

This ensures no opportunity slips through the cracks.

2. Document & Compliance Automation

Real estate is paperwork-heavy.

You can automate:

- document requests
- file storage
- reminders for renewals
- inspection timelines
- lease processes
- onboarding checklists

This eliminates mental fatigue and errors.

3. Communication Automation

Communication is the heaviest hidden time-cost in real estate.

Automate:

- buyer/seller intake
- tenant onboarding
- investor updates
- contractor scheduling
- PM coordination

Simple workflows free up your mind for strategic decisions.

4. Delegation & Human Automation

Automation is not only digital.

You also automate through:

- VAs
- standardized checklists
- recurring tasks
- outsourced tasks
- operational roles

This removes weight from your shoulders — permanently.

Expanding Wealth While Simplifying Life (*The Final Evolution*)

This is the endgame.

The point where:

- your systems work
- your alliances work
- your workflow works
- your decisions sharpen
- your stress decreases
- your income compounds

This is where real abundance begins.

Here's the model:

1. Build Systems That Run Themselves

Once a system works, improve it once…
then let it run repeatedly.

2. Use Delegation as a Wealth Strategy

Time is your most valuable asset.
Delegate everything that does not require your unique mind.

3. Focus Only on High-Value Decisions

Wealth accelerates when you stop doing low-value tasks and dedicate your mind to:

- relationships
- acquisitions
- capital
- strategy
- systems

4. Protect Your Energy

A tired investor loses money.
A clear investor multiplies it.

Simplifying life is not luxury — it is strategy.

Summary

Now you know the systems that make wealth predictable:

- Lead Systems
- Deal Analysis Systems
- Negotiation Systems
- Due Diligence Systems
- Renovation Systems
- Management Systems
- Review Loops
- Strategic Alliances
- Automation Frameworks
- Delegation Models
- Lifestyle Simplification Structure

This is more than a manual.

This is your complete roadmap.
Clear.
Actionable.
Repeatable.
Scalable.

When your systems align, your destination becomes inevitable.

Next up, **Chapter 14 — Resilience and the Empowered Wealth Mindset,** where we sharpen the mindset that keeps this entire machine alive — even when the storms hit.

CHAPTER 14

RESILIENCE AND THE EMPOWERED WEALTH MINDSET

Your scars don't define you.
They align you.
They don't just mark where you've been hurt.
They help you identify your character.

If you're reading this, chances are life has hit you a few times.
Losses.
Setbacks.
Deals that fell apart.
People who walked away.
Moments where you questioned who you were and where you were going.

This chapter is about those moments.
Not just about surviving them…
But becoming grateful for them.
Grateful for the experience.
Grateful for the lesson.
Grateful for the strength you discovered in the pain.

Because when you really understand resilience, you stop asking,
"Why did this happen to me?"
and you start realizing,
"This happened for me — to align me with who I'm meant to be."

That is the heart of an empowered wealth mindset.
Let's walk through it together.

Why Your Scars Don't Define You — They Align You

Every scar tells a story.
Some are visible.
Some are buried so deep in your heart that you forget they're even there…
until life presses on that exact spot.

When we're younger, we think the point of life is to get through without getting hurt.
No scars.
No mistakes.
No failures.
Then life happens.
We lose people we love.
We chase the wrong dreams.
We pick up habits that almost destroy us.
We trust people who fail us.
We make decisions that cost us time, money, and peace.

The natural reaction is shame.
Regret.
Wanting to erase chapters of our story.

Resilience starts with a different choice:
To be grateful not just that you survived…
but grateful for what the experience taught you.
Grateful for the clarity.

Grateful for the wake-up call.
Grateful for the strength you discovered when you had nothing left except Faith, Forgiveness, and Love.

Your scars become alignment when you decide:

- This does not lower my value.
- This deepens my character.
- This refines my vision.
- This sharpens my purpose.

Scars add character.
They don't erase who you are.
They reveal who you really are.

You are not your bankruptcy.
You are not your addiction.
You are not your worst investment, your worst decision, or your worst day.
You are who you chose to become in spite of it all.
That is alignment.

Becoming Stronger After Setbacks

(A Life Lived Through Reinvention)

To make this real, let me pull back the curtain on my own journey.

My father died of a drug overdose on Thanksgiving day, in our backyard, when I was eleven.
That loss shook my world.
I didn't know how to process grief at that age, so I threw myself into sports.
Football became my identity.
Intensity became my coping mechanism.

Then we moved to California.
New state.
New people.
New culture.
Once again, it was time to redefine myself.

So I became the best paper boy I could be.
Up before dawn.
Delivering newspapers, selling subscriptions.
Learning hustle, responsibility, and consistency without even realizing I was laying a foundation.

In my college years, I stepped into the car business and became obsessed with closing.
I wanted to be the best.
And I became very good at it.
I made more money in my twenties than I had any business making at that age.

That money was not a blessing.
Not the way I handled it.
I started following the same path my father did — drugs, self-destruction, and chaos.
Everything looked good on the outside.
On the inside, I was falling apart.

At twenty-six, I ended up in rehab.
That's where I had to redefine myself again.
This time, not as the closer.
Not as the car guy.
Not as the broken son of a broken man.
I had to reinvent myself as someone who could live clean.
Someone who could build a life without numbing out.
Someone who could face pain instead of running from it.

After a few years of learning how to live clean, I got into the furniture business.
Eventually, I became one of the top furniture salesmen and managers in the area.
Opening stores.
Training hundreds of salespeople.
Helping others make money and build careers.

And then… corporate burnout.
Long hours.
Constant pressure.
It was time to redefine myself again.

I opened a real estate investment company.
Started buying property across the United States.
Was featured in a real estate infomercial.

Soon I was traveling the country as a nationally recognized speaker, training investors for the International Association of Investors.

It looked like the dream.
Then the market crashed.
We lost everything.
The properties.
The house we lived in.
The vehicles.
We went bankrupt — $4.5 million.

That's not just a financial hit.
That's an identity hit.

Once again, I had a choice.
Collapse into shame.
Or redefine myself.

I became a real estate agent.
Worked my way back up.
Eventually opened my own brokerage: Solid Real Estate Solutions.
We still own and operate it today.

Then COVID hit.
The world shut down.
Real estate slowed.
Seminars stopped.
Time to redefine again.

That's when I leaned fully into hypnosis.
At first, it was stage shows and street hypnosis.
It was fun.
Entertaining.

A new way to connect with people.

Then I realized how powerful hypnosis really is when paired with healing.
When paired with neurolinguistic programming.
When paired with intention.
I recognized that I'd been using elements of influence, suggestion, and advanced communication my whole life — without having names for any of it.

So I went deeper.
Became a certified hypnotist.
Became an NLP practitioner.
Started studying the subconscious mind with serious focus.

That's when the FFL Modality was born out of the same principles that I have been since I was 26.
Faith.
Forgiveness.
Love.

It became the backbone of my healing.
The frame through which I understood my past.
The structure for how I wanted to live my future.

From that modality came the books:

- Infused Hypnosis: The Transformative Power of the FFL Modality — introducing FFL as a healing framework.
- Do You Sabotage Yourself Without Knowing It? — a deep dive into self-esteem through FFL.
- How Rocky the Lobster Outgrew His Shell — a children's story that carries the simplicity of FFL.

- Beyond Sales: The Neuroscience of Advanced Communication — merging hypnosis, NLP, and FFL into advanced communication.
- And now, this book — Real Estate Neuroscience: The Missing Piece the Gurus Don't Teach.

I also created the FFL Empower Yourself hypnosis series — 26 recordings that help people rewire their subconscious in specific areas of life.

Every hit life gave me forced me to redefine what I do…
and deepen who I am.

Looking back now, I can say this honestly:
I am grateful for all of it.
Not just grateful that I survived…
Grateful for the lessons.
Grateful for the perspective.
Grateful for the strength that only showed up when everything else fell away.

Life has blessed me with the exact experiences that I needed to experience to be exactly where I am today.
And I am grateful for who I am today.

That is resilience.
And that is available to you too.

Emotional Endurance as a Wealth Strategy

In real estate, people love to talk about:

- Cap rates

- Cash flow
- Equity
- Leveraging OPM
- Market cycles

All of that matters.
You've learned the mechanics throughout this book.

Yet there is one wealth skill almost nobody teaches:
Emotional endurance.

Deals fall apart.
Lenders change terms.
Partners back out.
Inspections reveal nightmares.
Cities change zoning.
Markets shift.
Tenants move out.

If your emotions collapse every time something goes sideways, your portfolio will never reach its potential.

Your ability to see the lesson in the pain is the same skill that allows you to see the opportunity in the problem.

When something goes wrong, most people say:
"This always happens to me."
"I knew it was too good to be true."
"I'm done with this."

A resilient investor asks:
"What is this trying to show me?"
"What pattern is being revealed?"

"What system needs to be improved?"
"How do I grow from this instead of shrinking from it?"

Emotional endurance looks like:

- Staying calm when a deal hits turbulence.
- Responding instead of reacting.
- Calmly making a decision and then acting on it.
- Being honest about mistakes without being crushed by them.
- Coming back to the table after a loss with more wisdom, not more bitterness.

Every challenge in this business carries two layers:

- The surface problem.
- The deeper lesson.

When you only focus on the surface problem, you get stuck in frustration.
When you commit to uncovering the lesson, you grow as a leader.
And when you grow as a leader, your wealth capacity expands.

Emotional endurance doesn't mean you "tough it out."
It means you train your mind and heart to:

- Feel the pain.
- Extract the lesson.
- Adjust the strategy.
- See the gratitude.
- Stay in the game.

This is a wealth strategy most people never develop.

Which is why most people never build the kind of legacy they're capable of.

Living the FFL Way: Faith, Forgiveness & Love

The FFL Modality is not a slogan for me.
It's not a marketing hook.
It's not an add-on.
It is my operating system.
My legacy.
The lens through which I see real estate, relationships, wealth and life.

In this final section, I want to show you how Faith, Forgiveness, and Love become the core of an empowered wealth mindset.

Faith — believing in a future you can't yet see

Fear lives in the future.
"What if this goes wrong?"
"What if the market turns?"
"What if I fail again?"

Faith lives in the same space — the future — yet it carries a different story:
"What if this works better than I imagined?"
"What if this setback is preparing me for something bigger?"
"What if I am more capable than I've ever given myself credit for?"

Faith is not denial.
Faith is not pretending risk doesn't exist.

Faith is the decision to believe in the possibility of a better outcome, even when you cannot see the whole path yet.

In real estate, Faith looks like:

- Believing there are still good deals, even in "tough" markets.
- Believing you can rebuild after a loss.
- Believing you can learn new skills at any stage of life.
- Believing you are worthy of abundance and alignment.

Faith doesn't erase risk.
Faith gives you the courage to move forward with wisdom in the presence of risk.

Forgiveness — releasing the weight of the past

Forgiveness is about the past.
Shame.
Guilt.
Regret.

The deal you should have taken.
The deal you should have walked away from.
The relationship you stayed in too long.
The money you wasted when you didn't know better.

If you don't forgive yourself, you drag all of that weight into every new opportunity.
You start to see the future through the lens of your past pain.

Forgiveness is not saying:

"It didn't matter."
Forgiveness is saying:
"It mattered deeply… and I'm done letting it control me."

In real estate and in life, Forgiveness looks like:

- Letting go of grudges against partners who wronged you, while learning the lesson about vetting better next time.
- Releasing the shame of financial mistakes so you can make strong decisions today.
- Accepting that you did the best you could with who you were and what you knew at the time.

Forgiveness frees up mental and emotional bandwidth.
Bandwidth you need for strategy, creativity, and clear decision-making.
Without Forgiveness, you keep re-litigating old deals in your head instead of creating new ones in the real world.

Love — presence, service, and how you show up now

Love is about the present.
How you treat people.
How you lead your team.
How you communicate with partners.
How you talk to yourself.

Love in business is not weakness.
It is strength with conscience.

Love looks like:

- Caring about your investors' outcomes, not just your own returns.
- Creating win–win–win structures where everyone at the table benefits.
- Treating tenants like human beings, not line items on a spreadsheet.
- Making strategies that protect your energy and integrity.
- Showing up with integrity, even when the conversation is hard.

When you operate from Love, people feel it.
They remember it.
They talk about it when you're not in the room.
That is how reputations are built.
That is how opportunities find you.

Because here's a truth you need to carry out of this book:
The newspapers I delivered, the cars I sold, the furniture I managed, the properties I bought and lost, the books I wrote —
None of that is the thing of ultimate value.

The real value is the person behind all of it.
The mind that keeps getting back up.
The heart that keeps opening again.
The spirit that keeps aligning with Faith, Forgiveness, and Love.

You are the real value.
Not the property.
Not the product.
Not the current deal on your desk.
You.
What you bring to the table.
The energy you carry into every room.

The decisions you make when nobody is watching.

You are the real asset.
FFL is the framework that keeps you aligned —
so wealth, opportunity, and aligned relationships can flow through you without destroying you.

Summary

(Resilience as your unfair advantage)

Now you understand:

Why your scars don't define you — they align you

- Scars add character, not shame.
- You can be grateful for the experience, not just survival.
- Your past pain refines your present purpose.

How to become stronger after setbacks

- Life will demand reinvention again and again.
- Each season of loss can reveal a deeper level of who you are.
- Redefining what you do is how you discover who you're meant to be.

Emotional endurance as a wealth strategy

- Your ability to see the lesson in the pain trains you to see opportunity in the problem.
- Emotional endurance keeps you in the game when others walk away.
- Calm, clarity, and perspective are assets more valuable than cash.

Living the FFL way

- Faith: believing in a future you can't yet see, instead of surrendering to fear.
- Forgiveness: releasing shame, guilt, and regret so your past doesn't choke your future.
- Love: choosing to show up with presence, integrity, and care in the present moment.

When you weave all of this together, something powerful happens:

You stop chasing deals…
and you start becoming the kind of person deals are drawn to.
You stop chasing validation…
and you start walking in alignment with who you really are.
You stop seeing your scars as disqualifiers…
and you start seeing them as the exact alignment you needed to become this version of yourself.

That is resilience.
That is an empowered wealth mindset.
That is the foundation that can hold the weight of everything you build.

And now, as we move into the conclusion, we're going to bring it all into one clear, unforgettable truth:
You've learned the science.
You've learned the strategies.
You've learned the systems.
Now it's time to talk about the most important asset in your entire portfolio.

Next up: Conclusion — The Real Asset.

CONCLUSION — THE REAL ASSET

You've made it to the end of this book.
But let me tell you something most people miss:

This is not the end.
This is the ignition point.

All the strategies…
All the systems…
All the neuroscience…
All the frameworks…
All the mindsets…
They're tools.

But tools don't build anything by themselves.
Tools need a builder.

And that builder…
is YOU.

Throughout this book, we talked about markets, negotiation, numbers, partnerships, alignment, influence, systems, deal creation, and emotional power…

But none of those things matter without the person holding them.

You.

You are the engine.
You are the compass.
You are the system.
You are the leverage.
You are the variable that changes the outcome.

YOU ARE THE REAL ASSET.

Not the property.
Not the market cycle.
Not the investor list.
Not the deal flow.
YOU.

Because here's the truth every wealthy person eventually discovers:

Real estate doesn't make you wealthy.
Who you become while building real estate makes you wealthy.

Your wealth expands only as fast as you expand.
Your portfolio grows only as far as your identity grows.
Your opportunities rise only as high as your energy rises.

You've learned the mechanics.
You've mastered the frameworks.
You've absorbed the systems.
You've strengthened your mindset.

Now you step into your next evolution.

The Journey You're Now On

By now you know:

- **Faith** shapes your future.
- **Forgiveness** frees your past.
- **Love** empowers your present.

- Alignment outperforms hustle.
- Emotional endurance outperforms talent.
- Consistency outperforms luck.
- Systems outpace chaos.
- Relationships scale faster than money.
- Character compounds more powerfully than cash flow.

And most importantly:
You don't need perfect conditions.
You don't need the "right market."
You don't need someone else's approval.
You don't need permission.

You are the permission.
You are the advantage.
You are the edge.

Everything else is just execution.

Your Scars Have Aligned You for This Moment

Look at everything you've survived:

The setbacks.
The losses.

The bankruptcies.
The detours.
The failures.
The wrong partnerships.
The heartbreaks.
The confusion.
The reinventions.

You've been tempered, not broken.
Shaped, not ruined.
Refined, not defeated.

Your scars weren't proof you were unworthy.
They were proof you were being prepared.

Prepared to see opportunity where others see problems.
Prepared to lead when others freeze.
Prepared to rise when others fall apart.
Prepared to align your life with something bigger, deeper, and more meaningful.

Prepared to build wealth from a place of integrity, influence, and power — not fear.

Everything you went through was training.
Every chapter of your life was pointing you here.

One aligned decision away from a completely different trajectory.

The World Needs Who You're Becoming

Real estate is not just about profit.

It's about impact.

- Families need homes.
- Investors need leaders they can trust.
- Communities need problem solvers.
- Partners need clarity and alignment.
- People need examples of resilience.

You are that example now.

Not because you're perfect.
But because you're *intentional.*

Not because you never fall.
But because you rise with purpose.

Not because you never doubt.
But because you move with Faith anyway.

Not because you're fearless.
But because you refuse to let fear drive.

The world needs people like you —
people committed to growing, leading, aligning, and lifting others.

People who don't just build portfolios…
but build character, unity, and transformation in the process.

Your Next Chapter Starts Now

This book opened the door.

But the walk — the journey — the transformation — that's entirely yours.

You now have:

- The frameworks
- The negotiation mastery
- The emotional fortitude
- The deal-making intelligence
- The alignment strategies
- The FFL operating system
- The wealth architecture
- The resilience to endure anything
- The vision to build everything

And with all of that inside you, the only question left is:

What will you do with it?

You can close this book and go back to the old way…
or you can step into the identity that's been calling you forward since the very beginning.

The identity of someone who doesn't just survive life —
but shapes it.
Directs it.
Influences it.
Builds it.
Leads it.
Elevates it.

The identity of someone who understands:

Wealth isn't what you stack.
Wealth is what you become.

One Final Truth Before You Turn the Page

You were never missing resources.
You were only missing alignment.

Now you have it.

You were never missing potential.
You were only missing structure.

Now you have it.

You were never missing opportunity.
You were only missing the lens to see it.

Now you have it.

You were never missing worth.
You were only missing the belief in it.

Now you have it.

You are the real asset.
Protect it.
Grow it.
Honor it.
Lead through it.
And let wealth — real wealth — flow from that aligned version of you.

Because when you lead with Faith,
move with Forgiveness,
and live with Love…

You become unstoppable.
And the world…
is waiting for the impact only YOU can make.

ABOUT THE AUTHOR

Jason Gobeli is the Founder and CEO of **FFL Neuro-Communications, LLC**, a company dedicated to advancing human potential through intentional presence, advanced communication, and subconscious transformation. His work blends neuroscience-driven communication, hypnosis, NLP, emotional alignment, and wealth psychology into a unified system that helps people live with greater purpose, clarity, and impact.

A real estate broker, investor, hypnotist, neuro-communication expert, speaker, and author, Jason brings more than **40 years of combined experience** across sales, leadership, real estate, negotiation, and transformational communication. His unique ability to merge strategy with human behavior has positioned him as a trusted guide for individuals seeking growth—professionally, emotionally, and financially.

Jason is the creator of the **FFL Modality — Faith, Forgiveness, and Love**, the foundational operating system behind all of his work. From advanced communication to emotional healing to wealth creation, his FFL framework serves as a compass for alignment, resilience, and intentional living. It is woven into his books, seminars, hypnosis work, stage performances, and corporate trainings.

He is the owner of **Solid Real Estate Solutions**, a California brokerage grounded in the philosophy, "We Solve Real Estate Problems."

He is also a partner in **3D Real Estate Developers**, a company focused on innovation, 3D-printed housing, and accessible housing solutions across the U.S.

Through **Go Under Hypnosis**, he helps individuals transform subconscious patterns, breakthrough emotional blocks, and create real alignment in their lives.

Jason has been **clean since 1989** and has spent **decades serving the recovery community**—sponsoring countless individuals, volunteering in prisons, and helping people rebuild their lives with dignity, structure, and hope. His long-term commitment to service is a defining part of his character and the foundation of his message.

Married for over **30 years**, Jason is a devoted husband, father of three, and grandfather of one. Family remains the heart of his purpose and the anchor of his values.

He is the author of multiple books, including:

- Infused Hypnosis: The Transformative Power of the FFL Modality
- Do You Sabotage Yourself Without Knowing It?
- How Rocky the Lobster Outgrew His Shell
- Beyond Sales: The Neuroscience of Advanced Communication
- Real Estate Neuroscience: The Missing Piece the Gurus Don't Teach

No matter the platform—books, seminars, real estate, hypnosis, or private coaching—Jason's mission remains the same:

To help people awaken their potential, elevate their communication, and build lives aligned with Faith, Forgiveness, and Love.

Connect With Jason

FFL Neuro-Communications, LLC
"Intentional Presence with Purpose"
www.neuro-communications.com

Solid Real Estate Solutions — "We Solve Real Estate Problems"
www.solidresolutions.com

3D Real Estate Developers — "We Print Homes"
www.3D-guys.com

Go Under Hypnosis (Jason Gobeli, Hypnotist) — "Empower Yourself: Envision. Create. Inspire. Transform."
www.go-under.com

Or simply go to his direct webpage
www.JasonGobeli.com

www.ingramcontent.com/pod-product-compliance
Lightning Source LLC
LaVergne TN
LVHW052314200926
848481LV00002B/567